"Brennan Manning does a masterful job of blowing the dust off of shop-worn theology and allowing God's grace to do what only God's grace can do—amaze."

—MAX LUCADO
Bestselling author of
Come Thirsty and *The Gift for All People*

"I found deep comfort in realizing that Jesus loves even me, a ragamuffin, just as I am and not as I should be; that he accepts me, though I am most unacceptable. I came to this book hungry; I tasted and saw afresh that our God truly is good and that He is, after all, for us."

—MICHAEL CARD
Musician, recording artist, and author

"So much religion is conveyed to us as bad news or bland news that we are immensely grateful when it is spoken freshly as good news. This is a zestful and accurate portrayal that tells us unmistakably that the gospel is good, dazzlingly good."

—EUGENE PETERSON
Author of *The Message*

THE
RAGAMUFFIN
GOSPEL

BRENNAN MANNING

Multnomah Books

THE RAGAMUFFIN GOSPEL
published by Multnomah Books
A Division of Random House, Inc.

The author is represented by Alive Communications, Inc.,
7680 Goddard St., Suite 200, Colorado Springs, CO 80920

© 1990, 2000, 2005 by Brennan Manning

International Standard Book Number: 1-59052-540-X

Cover photo by Ben Pearson Photography
Interior design and typeset by Katherine Lloyd, The DESK

Unless otherwise indicated, Scripture quotations are from:
The Jerusalem Bible © 1966 by Darton, Longman & Todd, Ltd. and
Doubleday & Company, Inc. All rights reserved.

Other Scripture quotations are from:
The Message © 1993, 1994, 1995, 1996, 2000, 2001, 2002.
Used by permission of NavPress Publishing Group.
The New American Bible (NAB) with Revised New Testament
© 1986 and Revised Psalms © 1991 by the Confraternity of Christian
Doctrine. All Rights Reserved.

Multnomah is a trademark of Multnomah Publishers
and is registered in the U.S. Patent and Trademark Office.
The colophon is a trademark of Multnomah Publishers.

Printed in the United States of America

For information:
MULTNOMAH BOOKS
12265 ORACLE BOULEVARD, SUITE 200
COLORADO SPRINGS, CO 80921

07 08 09 10—48 47 46 45

Contents

FOREWORD

by Michael W. Smith

J probably first heard the word *ragamuffin* while sitting in school listening with less-than-rapt attention to an English teacher reading from a Dickens novel or some other three-inch-thick book. The word really didn't grab my attention.

The next time the word came into my life was through music. My friend and fellow singer-songwriter Rich Mullins assembled a ragtag crew of musician friends and dubbed them the Ragamuffin Band. They celebrated the unconditional love of God, and the more their lives and music exemplified the idea of ragamuffinness, the more intriguing and appealing that word became to me.

Then I discovered Brennan Manning's *The Ragamuffin Gospel,* the same rich treasure chest where Rich had found the word. The first time I sat down with the book, I devoured it. Between the words of its pages I found a new freedom. I

discovered how little I had to do to deserve and receive the love
of God and that He loved me more than I had ever imagined.
Suddenly, instead of fearing and denying all of my real or
imagined shortcomings, I could embrace my humanness. I
could see God pursuing me through it and in spite of it.

Here was the purest picture I'd ever seen of God's relentless
pursuit of His raggedy creation. Not that I could sin more so
grace might abound (see Romans 6:15), but grace abounded
more because I could find it in the darkness as much as in the
light. God wanted me just as I am. I am loved. Brennan took
every cliché I had ever spouted or had had spouted at me and
turned it into gold.

Ever since that first magical moment of discovery when
the radical message of the unconditional, immeasurable, life-
changing love of God jumped out at me from the pages of *The
Ragamuffin Gospel,* I couldn't wait to tell everyone about it. I
can't even remember how many copies I have given away. Much
like the gospel, once it captures your heart, you can't wait to
have it embrace everyone else's.

Since then I've met hundreds of other *Ragamuffin* fans. Our
stories are all pretty much the same. For the first time in our
walks of faith, we found something so old and so basic that it
seemed stunningly new and profound. We are all ragamuffins,
and we are all endlessly wrapped in God's arms of grace.

Recently I attended a two-day retreat led by Brennan
Manning. Brennan's gentle spirit was the perfect reflection of
what I needed to learn, and the retreat was a refreshing time
of reminding us of the truth that God is always *with* us and
for us. The touchstone was, "Abba, I belong to you." Lovingly,

Brennan drilled into us that message—the father-love and acceptance we are so prone to forget. I found myself repeating those words over and over again long after the weekend had passed. It was not unlike the weeks after I first read *The Ragamuffin Gospel.* I found myself marveling out loud at those wonderful, powerful glimpses of the Creator and His unfathomable love for me.

Some books are a great read. Some have taught me lifelong lessons that have made my life more of what I'm sure God intended it to be. And, of course, some have impressed my friends but gathered dust on my shelves. *The Ragamuffin Gospel* was and is different. It transformed me. I will never be the same.

Don't let the cover fool you: This is a dangerous book. It will shake you to your core and shuffle every idea you've neatly arranged in your brain. As for me, I welcomed the intrusion.

Thank you, Brennan, for awakening the ragamuffin in all of us. And to you lucky readers about to plunge in, drink deeply. You are in for an incredible experience!

Testimony

by Rich Mullins

I owe Brennan Manning thirty dollars for lecture tapes I bought from him on an IOU. I'm not writing this testimony because of that debt. I simply mention it because indebtedness is a condition indicative of ragamuffins—a condition we all share, until we lose ourselves in the liberating, healing, invigorating truth to which these pages bear testimony.

My introduction to Brennan Manning's work came on a drive south from Manhattan, Kansas, through the edge of the Flinthills. It is a beautiful drive, best accompanied by the music of Aaron Copeland. Or by pure silence. When a friend put a tape of one of Manning's lectures in my truck's tape player, I objected. But my friend said, "Just give it ten minutes."

Five minutes later, I steered the truck onto the shoulder of the road. My eyes were so full of tears, I could not see to drive.

I have attended church regularly since I was less than a week old. I've listened to sermons about virtue, sermons against vice. I have heard about money, time management, tithing, abstinence, and generosity. I've listened to thousands of sermons. But I could count on one hand the number that were a simple proclamation of the gospel of Christ.

That proclamation is the message I heard that day. And it did what the gospel can't help but do: It broke the power of mere "moralistic religiosity" in my life and revived a deeper acceptance that had long ago withered in me.

In our society, we tend to swear unyielding allegiance to a rigid position, confusing that action with finding an authentic connection to a life-giving Spirit. We miss the gospel of Christ: the good news that, although the holy and all-powerful God knows we are dust, He still stoops to breathe into us the breath of life—to bring to our wounds the balm of acceptance and love. No other author has articulated this message more simply or beautifully than Brennan Manning.

I owe Brennan Manning thirty dollars, and I expect to get it to him soon. But I owe him an even bigger debt for the freedom he helped me find through this book . . . and the greatest debt of all to the God whose grace extends to—and especially for—the ragamuffins of this world.

ACKNOWLEDGMENTS

*E*velyn Underhill said, "Spiritual reading is, or at least can be, second only to prayer as a developer and support of the inner life." And *The Message of the Wesleys* contains this striking sentence: "It cannot be that people should grow in grace unless they give themselves to reading." Surely a gracious God provides for the illiterate in other ways, but for most of us, the Scriptures and varied spiritual writings guide us to a deeper understanding of the truth that sets us free.

Humbly and happily, I express my gratitude to several Christian authors upon whom I have relied for deeper insight into Jesus Christ and the gospel of grace: Edward Schillebeeckx, Walter Burghardt, Hans Küng, Donald McCullough, Leonard Foley, Eugene Kennedy, Albert Nolan, Jaroslav Pelikan, Sean Caulfield, Anthony De Mello, Lloyd Ogilvie, and others quoted in these pages.

Finally, my thanks to John van Diest and Liz Heaney, whose enthusiasm over the first few pages of this book fueled the desire to finish it.

A Word Before

The Ragamuffin Gospel was written with a specific reading audience in mind.

This book is not for the superspiritual.

It is not for muscular Christians who have made John Wayne, and not Jesus, their hero.

It is not for academics who would imprison Jesus in the ivory tower of exegesis.

It is not for noisy, feel-good folks who manipulate Christianity into a naked appeal to emotion.

It is not for hooded mystics who want magic in their religion.

It is not for Alleluia Christians who live only on the mountaintop and have never visited the valley of desolation.

It is not for the fearless and tearless.

It is not for red-hot zealots who boast with the rich young ruler of the Gospels, "All these commandments I have kept from my youth."

It is not for the complacent who hoist over their shoulders

a tote bag of honors, diplomas, and good works, actually believing they have it made.

It is not for legalists who would rather surrender control of their souls to rules than run the risk of living in union with Jesus.

If anyone is still reading along, *The Ragamuffin Gospel* was written for the bedraggled, beat-up, and burnt-out.

It is for the sorely burdened who are still shifting the heavy suitcase from one hand to the other.

It is for the wobbly and weak-kneed who know they don't have it all together and are too proud to accept the handout of amazing grace.

It is for inconsistent, unsteady disciples whose cheese is falling off their cracker.

It is for poor, weak, sinful men and women with hereditary faults and limited talents.

It is for earthen vessels who shuffle along on feet of clay.

It is for the bent and the bruised who feel that their lives are a grave disappointment to God.

It is for smart people who know they are stupid and honest disciples who admit they are scalawags.

The Ragamuffin Gospel is a book I wrote for myself and anyone who has grown weary and discouraged along the Way.

—Brennan Manning

Chapter One

SOMETHING IS
RADICALLY WRONG

On a blustery October night in a church outside Minneapolis, several hundred believers had gathered for a three-day seminar. I began with a one-hour presentation on the gospel of grace and the reality of salvation. Using Scripture, story, symbolism, and personal experience, I focused on the total sufficiency of the redeeming work of Jesus Christ on Calvary. The service ended with a song and a prayer.

Leaving the church by a side door, the pastor turned to his associate and fumed, "Humph, that airhead didn't say one thing about what we have to do to earn our salvation!"

Something is radically wrong.

The bending of the mind by the powers of this world has

twisted the gospel of grace into religious bondage and distorted the image of God into an eternal, small-minded bookkeeper. The Christian community resembles a Wall Street exchange of works wherein the elite are honored and the ordinary ignored. Love is stifled, freedom shackled, and self-righteousness fastened. The institutional church has become a wounder of the healers rather than a healer of the wounded.

Put bluntly, the American church today accepts grace in theory but denies it in practice. We say we believe that the fundamental structure of reality is grace, not works—but our lives refute our faith. By and large, the gospel of grace is neither proclaimed, understood, nor lived. Too many Christians are living in the house of fear and not in the house of love.

Our culture has made the word *grace* impossible to understand. We resonate to slogans such as:

"There's no free lunch."

"You get what you deserve."

"You want money? Work for it."

"You want love? Earn it."

"You want mercy? Show you deserve it."

"Do unto others before they do unto you."

"Watch out for welfare lines, the shiftless street people, free hot dogs at school, affluent students with federal loans—it's a con game."

"By all means, give others what they deserve but not one penny more."

A friend told me she overheard a pastor say to a child, "God loves good little boys." As I listen to sermons with their pointed emphasis on personal effort—no pain, no gain—I get the impression that a do-it-yourself spirituality is the American fashion.

Though the Scriptures insist on God's initiative in the work of salvation—that by grace we are saved, that the Tremendous Lover has taken to the chase—our spirituality often starts with self, not God. Personal responsibility has replaced personal response. We talk about acquiring virtue as if it were a skill that can be attained, like good handwriting or a well-grooved golf swing. In the penitential seasons we focus on overcoming our weaknesses, getting rid of our hang-ups, and reaching Christian maturity. We sweat through various spiritual exercises as if they were designed to produce a Christian Charles Atlas. Though lip service is paid to the gospel of grace, many Christians live as if only personal discipline and self-denial will mold the perfect me. The emphasis is on what I do rather than on what God is doing. In this curious process God is a benign old spectator in the bleachers who cheers when I show up for morning quiet time. We transfer the Horatio Alger legend of the self-made man into our relationship with God. As we read Psalm 123, "Like the eyes of the servant on the hands of his master, like the eyes of a maid on the hands of her mistress," we experience a vague sense of existential guilt. Our eyes are not on God. At heart we are practicing Pelagians. We believe that we can pull ourselves up by our bootstraps—indeed, we can do it ourselves.

Sooner or later we are confronted with the painful truth of our inadequacy and insufficiency. Our security is shattered and our bootstraps are cut. Once the fervor has passed, weakness and infidelity appear. We discover our inability to add even a single inch to our spiritual stature. There begins a long winter of discontent that eventually flowers into gloom, pessimism, and a subtle despair—subtle because it goes unrecognized, unnoticed, and therefore unchallenged. It takes the form of boredom, drudgery. We are overcome by the ordinariness of life, by daily duties done over and over again. We secretly admit that the call of Jesus is too demanding, that surrender to the Spirit is beyond our reach. We start acting like everyone else. Life takes on a joyless, empty quality. We begin to resemble the leading character in Eugene O'Neill's play *The Great God Brown:* "Why am I afraid to dance, I who love music and rhythm and grace and song and laughter? Why am I afraid to live, I who love life and the beauty of flesh and the living colors of the earth and sky and sea? Why am I afraid to love, I who love love?"[1]

Something is radically wrong.

Our huffing and puffing to impress God, our scrambling for brownie points, our thrashing about trying to fix ourselves while hiding our pettiness and wallowing in guilt are nauseating to God and are a flat denial of the gospel of grace.

Our approach to the Christian life is as absurd as the enthusiastic young man who had just received his plumber's license and was taken to see Niagara Falls. He studied it for a minute and then said, "I think I can fix this."[2]

The word itself, *grace,* has become trite and debased through misuse and overuse. It does not move us the way it moved our early Christian ancestors. In some European countries certain high ecclesiastical officials are still called "Your Grace." Sportswriters spoke of Michael Jordan's "easy grace," while business mogul Donald Trump has been described as "lacking in grace." A new perfume appears with "Grace" on the label, and a child's report card is called a "disgrace." The word has lost its raw, imaginative power.

Fyodor Dostoyevsky caught the shock and scandal of the gospel of grace when he wrote:

> At the last Judgment Christ will say to us, "Come, you also! Come, drunkards! Come, weaklings! Come, children of shame!" And he will say to us: "Vile beings, you who are in the image of the beast and bear his mark, but come all the same, you as well." And the wise and prudent will say, "Lord, why do you welcome them?" And he will say: "If I welcome them, you wise men, if I welcome them, you prudent men, it is because not one of them has ever been judged worthy." And he will stretch out his arms, and we will fall at his feet, and we will cry out sobbing, and then we will understand all, we will understand the Gospel of grace! Lord, your Kingdom come![3]

I believe the Reformation actually began the day Martin Luther was praying over the meaning of Paul's assertion that the gospel reveals the righteousness of God to us—it shows how faith leads to faith. In other words, the righteous shall find life through faith (see Romans 1:17). Like many Christians today, Luther wrestled through the night with this core question: How could the gospel of Christ be truly called "good news" if God is a righteous judge who rewards the good and punishes the evil? Did

Jesus really have to come to reveal that terrifying message? How could the revelation of God in Christ Jesus be accurately called "news" since the Old Testament carried the same theme, or for that matter, "good" with the threat of punishment hanging like a dark cloud over the valley of history?

But as Jaroslav Pelikan notes:

> Luther suddenly broke through to the insight that the "righteousness of God" that Paul spoke of in this passage was not the righteousness by which God was righteous in himself (that would be passive righteousness) but the righteousness by which, for the sake of Jesus Christ, God made sinners righteous (that is, active righteousness) through the forgiveness of sins in justification. When he discovered that, Luther said it was as though the very gates of Paradise had been opened to him.[4]

What a stunning truth!

"Justification by grace through faith" is the theologian's learned phrase for what Chesterton once called "the furious love of God." He is not moody or capricious; He knows no seasons of change. He has a single relentless stance toward us: He loves us. He is the only God man has ever heard of who loves sinners. False gods—the gods of human manufacturing—despise sinners, but the Father of Jesus loves all, no matter what they do. But of course, this is almost too incredible for us to accept. Nevertheless, the central affirmation of the Reformation stands: Through no merit of ours, but by His mercy, we have been restored to a right relationship with God through the life, death, and resurrection of His beloved Son. This is the Good News, the gospel of grace.

With his characteristic *joie de vivre,* Robert Capon puts it this way:

> The Reformation was a time when men went blind, staggering drunk because they had discovered, in the dusty basement of late medievalism, a whole cellarful of fifteen-hundred-year-old, two-hundred-proof grace—of bottle after bottle of pure distillate of Scripture, one sip of which would convince anyone that God saves us single-handedly. The word of the gospel—after all those centuries of trying to lift yourself into heaven by worrying about the perfection of your bootstraps—suddenly turned out to be a flat announcement that the saved were home before they started... Grace has to be drunk straight: no water, no ice, and certainly no ginger ale; neither goodness, nor badness, nor the flowers that bloom in the spring of super spirituality could be allowed to enter into the case.[5]

Matthew 9:9–13 captures a lovely glimpse of the gospel of grace:

> As Jesus was walking on from there he saw a man named Matthew sitting at the tax office, and he said to him, "Follow me." And he got up and followed him. Now while he was at table in the house it happened that a number of tax collectors and sinners came to sit at the table with Jesus and his disciples. When the Pharisees

saw this, they said to his disciples, "Why does your master eat with tax collectors and sinners?" When he heard this he replied, "It is not the healthy who need the doctor, but the sick. Go and learn the meaning of the words: Mercy is what pleases me, not sacrifice. And indeed I came to call not the upright, but sinners."

Here is revelation bright as the evening star: Jesus comes for sinners, for those as outcast as tax collectors and for those caught up in squalid choices and failed dreams. He comes for corporate executives, street people, superstars, farmers, hookers, addicts, IRS agents, AIDS victims, and even used-car salesmen. Jesus not only talks with these people but dines with them—fully aware that His table fellowship with sinners will raise the eyebrows of religious bureaucrats who hold up the robes and insignia of their authority to justify their condemnation of the truth and their rejection of the gospel of grace.

This passage should be read, reread, and memorized. Every Christian generation tries to dim the blinding brightness of its meaning because the gospel seems too good to be true. We think salvation belongs to the proper and pious, to those who stand at a safe distance from the back alleys of existence, clucking their judgments at those who have been soiled by life. In the name of Grace, what has been the verdict of the Christian community on the stained life of the late Rock Hudson? To the disclosure (the $4.5 million settlement to his lover Marc Christian notwithstanding) that he called a priest to his deathbed, confessed his sins, and cried out to God for forgiveness?

Jesus, who forgave the sins of the paralytic (thereby claiming divine power), proclaims that He has invited sinners and not the self-righteous to His table. The Greek verb used here, *kalein,* has the sense of inviting an honored guest to dinner. In effect, Jesus says the kingdom of His Father is not a subdivision for the self-righteous nor for those who feel they possess the state secret of salvation. The kingdom is not an exclusive, well-trimmed suburb with snobbish rules about who can live there. No, it is for a larger, homelier, less self-conscious caste of people who understand they are sinners because they have experienced the yaw and pitch of moral struggle.

These are the sinner-guests invited by Jesus to closeness with Him around the banquet table. It remains a startling story to those who never understand that the men and women who are truly filled with light are those who have gazed deeply into the darkness of their imperfect existence. Perhaps it was after meditating on this passage that Morton Kelsey wrote, "The church is not a museum for saints but a hospital for sinners."

The Good News means we can stop lying to ourselves. The sweet sound of amazing grace saves us from the necessity of self-deception. It keeps us from denying that though Christ was victorious, the battle with lust, greed, and pride still rages within us. As a sinner who has been redeemed, I can acknowledge that I am often unloving, irritable, angry, and resentful with those closest to me. When I go to church I can leave my white hat at home and admit I have failed. God not only loves me as I am, but also knows me as I am. Because of this I don't need to apply spiritual cosmetics to make myself presentable to Him. I can accept ownership of my poverty and powerlessness and neediness.

As C. S. Lewis says in *The Four Loves,* "Grace substitutes a full, childlike and delighted acceptance of our need, a joy in total dependence. The good man is sorry for the sins which have increased his need. He is not entirely sorry for the fresh need they have produced."

As the gospel of grace lays hold of us, something is radically right. We are living in truth and reality. We become as honest as the ninety-two-year-old priest who was venerated by everybody in town for his holiness. He was also a member of the Rotary Club. Every time the club met, he would be there, always on time and always seated in his favorite spot in a corner of the room.

One day the priest disappeared. It was as if he had vanished into thin air. The townsfolk searched all over and could find no trace of him. But the following month, when the Rotary Club met, he was there as usual sitting in his corner.

"Father," everyone cried, "where have you been?"

"I just served a thirty-day sentence in prison."

"In prison?" they cried. "Father, you couldn't hurt a fly. What happened?"

"It's a long story," said the priest, "but briefly, this is what happened. I bought myself a train ticket to go into the city. I was standing on the platform waiting for the train to arrive when this stunningly beautiful girl appears on the arm of a policeman. She looked at me, turned to the cop and said, 'He did it. I'm certain he's the one who did it.' Well, to tell you the truth, I was so flattered I pleaded guilty."[6]

There's a touch of vanity in even the holiest men and women. They see no reason to deny it. And they know that reality bites back if it isn't respected.

When I get honest, I admit I am a bundle of paradoxes. I believe and I doubt, I hope and get discouraged, I love and I hate, I feel bad about feeling good, I feel guilty about not feeling guilty. I am trusting and suspicious. I am honest and I still play games. Aristotle said I am a rational animal; I say I am an angel with an incredible capacity for beer.

To live by grace means to acknowledge my whole life story, the light side and the dark. In admitting my shadow side, I learn who I am and what God's grace means. As Thomas Merton put it, "A saint is not someone who is good but who experiences the goodness of God."

The gospel of grace nullifies our adulation of televangelists, charismatic superstars, and local church heroes. It obliterates the two-class citizenship theory operative in many American churches. For grace proclaims the awesome truth that all is gift. All that is good is ours, not by right, but by the sheer bounty of a gracious God. While there is much we may have earned—our degree, our salary, our home and garden, and a good night's sleep—all this is possible only because we have been given so much: life itself, eyes to see and hands to touch, a mind to shape ideas, and a heart to beat with love. We have been given God in our souls and Christ in our flesh. We have the power to believe where others deny, to hope where others despair, to love where others hurt. This and so much more is sheer gift; it is not reward for our faithfulness, our generous disposition, or our heroic life of prayer. Even our fidelity is a gift. "If we but turn to God," said St. Augustine, "that itself is a gift of God." My deepest awareness of myself is that I am deeply loved by Jesus Christ and I have done nothing to earn it or deserve it.

In my ministry as a vagabond evangelist, I have extolled certain saints and contemporary Christians, speaking of at what cost they have struggled to surpass lesser men and women. O God, what madness I have preached in sermons! The Good News of the gospel of grace cries out: We are all, equally, privileged but unentitled beggars at the door of God's mercy!

Besides, as Henri Nouwen notes, the greater part of God's work in the world may go unnoticed. There are a number of people who have become famous or widely known for their ministries, but much of God's saving activity in our history could remain completely unknown. That is a mystery difficult to grasp in an age that attaches so much importance to publicity. We tend to think that the more people know and talk about something, the more important it must be.

In Luke 18, a rich young man comes to Jesus, asking what he must *do* to inherit eternal life. He wants to be in the spotlight. It is no coincidence that Luke juxtaposes the passage of Jesus and the children immediately preceding the verses on the young aristocrat. Children contrast with the rich man simply because there is no question of their having yet been able to merit anything. Jesus' point is, there is nothing that any of us can do to inherit the kingdom. We must simply receive it like little children. And little children haven't done anything. The New Testament world was not sentimental about children and had no illusion about any pretended innate goodness in them. Jesus is not suggesting that heaven is a huge playground for Cajun infants. Children are our model because they have no claim on heaven. If they are close to God, it is because they are incompetent, not because they are innocent. If they receive anything, it can only be as a gift.

Paul writes in Ephesians, "Because it is by grace that you have been saved, through faith; not by anything of your own, but by a gift from God, not by anything that you have done, so that nobody can claim the credit" (2:8–9).

If a random sampling of one thousand American Christians were taken today, the majority would define faith as belief in the existence of God. In earlier times it did not take faith to believe that God existed—almost everybody took that for granted. Rather, faith had to do with one's relationship to God— whether one trusted in God. The difference between faith as "belief in something that may or may not exist" and faith as "trusting in God" is enormous. The first is a matter of the head, the second a matter of the heart. The first can leave us unchanged; the second intrinsically brings change.[7]

Such is the faith described by Paul Tillich in his famous work *The Shaking of the Foundations:*

> Grace strikes us when we are in great pain and restless-
> ness. It strikes us when we walk through the dark valley
> of a meaningless and empty life… It strikes us when,
> year after year, the longed-for perfection does not appear,
> when the old compulsions reign within us as they have
> for decades, when despair destroys all joy and courage.
> Sometimes at that moment a wave of light breaks into
> our darkness, and it is as though a voice were saying:
> "You are accepted. You are accepted, accepted by that
> which is greater than you, and the name of which you

do not know. Do not ask for the name now; perhaps you will find it later. Do not try to do anything now; perhaps later you will do much. Do not seek for anything, do not perform anything, do not intend anything. Simply accept the fact that you are accepted." If that happens to us, we experience grace.[8]

And Grace calls out, *You are not just a disillusioned old man who may die soon, a middle-aged woman stuck in a job and desperately wanting to get out, a young person feeling the fire in the belly begin to grow cold. You may be insecure, inadequate, mistaken, or potbellied. Death, panic, depression, and disillusionment may be near you. But you are not just that. You are accepted.* Never confuse your perception of yourself with the mystery that you really are accepted.

Paul writes, "The Lord said, 'My grace is enough for you: my power is at its best in weakness.' So I shall be very happy to make my weaknesses my special boast so that the power of Christ may stay over me" (2 Corinthians 12:9). Whatever our failings may be, we need not lower our eyes in the presence of Jesus. Unlike Quasimodo, the hunchback of Notre Dame, we need not hide all that is ugly and repulsive in us. Jesus comes not for the super-spiritual but for the wobbly and the weak-kneed who know they don't have it all together, and who are not too proud to accept the handout of amazing grace. As we glance up, we are astonished to find the eyes of Jesus open with wonder, deep with understanding, and gentle with compassion.

Something is radically wrong when the local church rejects a person accepted by Jesus—when a harsh, judgmental, and unforgiving sentence is passed on homosexuals; when a divorcée is denied communion; when the child of a prostitute is refused baptism; when an unlaicized priest is forbidden the sacraments. Jesus comes to the ungodly, even on Sunday morning. His coming ends ungodliness and makes us worthy. Otherwise, we are establishing at the heart of Christianity an utterly ungodly and unworthy preoccupation with works.

Jesus sat down at table with anyone who wanted to be present, including those who were banished from decent homes. In the sharing of a meal they received consideration instead of the expected condemnation. A merciful acquittal instead of a hasty verdict of guilty. Amazing grace instead of universal disgrace. Here is a very practical demonstration of the law of grace—a new chance in life.

Any church that will not accept that it consists of sinful men and women, and exists for them, implicitly rejects the gospel of grace. As Hans Küng says:

> It deserves neither God's mercy nor men's trust. The church must constantly be aware that its faith is weak, its knowledge dim, its profession of faith halting, that there is not a single sin or failing which it has not in one way or another been guilty of. *And though it is true that the church must always dissociate itself from sin, it can never have any excuse for keeping any sinners at a distance.* If the church remains self-righteously aloof from failures, irreligious and immoral people, it cannot enter justified into God's kingdom. But if it is constantly aware of its guilt and sin, it can live in joyous awareness of

forgiveness. The promise has been given to it that anyone who humbles himself will be exalted.[9]

The story goes that a public sinner was excommunicated and forbidden entry to the church. He took his woes to God. "They won't let me in, Lord, because I am a sinner."

"What are you complaining about?" said God. "They won't let Me in either."

Often hobbling through our church doors on Sunday morning comes grace on crutches—sinners still unable to throw away their false supports and stand upright in the freedom of the children of God. Yet their mere presence in the church on Sunday morning is a flickering candle representing a desire to maintain contact with God. To douse the flame is to plunge them into a world of spiritual darkness.

There is a myth flourishing in the church today that has caused incalculable harm: once converted, fully converted. In other words, once I accept Jesus Christ as my Lord and Savior, an irreversible, sinless future beckons. Discipleship will be an untarnished success story; life will be an unbroken upward spiral toward holiness. Tell that to poor Peter who, after three times professing his love for Jesus on the beach and after receiving the fullness of the Spirit at Pentecost, was still jealous of Paul's apostolic success.

Often I have been asked, "Brennan, how is it possible that you became an alcoholic after you got saved?" It is possible because I got battered and bruised by loneliness and failure; because I got discouraged, uncertain, guilt-ridden, and took my eyes off Jesus. Because the Christ-encounter did not transfigure me into an angel. Because justification by grace through faith means I have been set in right relationship with God, not made the equivalent of a patient etherized on a table.

We want ever-sharp spirituality—push, pull, click, click, one saint that quick—and attempt to cultivate a particular virtue at a given point in time. Prudence in January, humility in February, fortitude in March, temperance in April. Score cards are provided for toting up gains and losses. The losses should diminish if you expect to meet charity in May. Sometimes May never comes. For many Christians, life is a long January.

According to an ancient Christian legend, a saint once knelt down and prayed, "Dear God, I have only one desire in life. Give me the grace of never offending You again."

When God heard this, He started laughing out loud. "That's what they all ask for. But if I granted everyone this grace, tell Me, whom would I forgive?"

Because salvation is by grace through faith, I believe that among the countless number of people standing in front of the throne and in front of the Lamb, dressed in white robes and holding palms in their hands (see Revelation 7:9), I shall see the prostitute from the Kit-Kat Ranch in Carson City, Nevada, who tearfully told me she could find no other employment to support her two-year-old son. I shall see the woman who had an abortion and is haunted by guilt and remorse but did the best she could faced with grueling alternatives; the businessman besieged with debt who sold his integrity in a series of desperate transactions; the insecure clergyman addicted to being liked, who never challenged his people from the pulpit and longed for unconditional love; the sexually abused teen molested by his father and now selling his body on the street, who, as he falls asleep each night after his last "trick," whispers the name of the unknown God he learned about in Sunday school; the deathbed convert who for decades had his cake and ate it, broke every law of God and man, wallowed in lust, and raped the earth.

"But how?" we ask.

Then the voice says, "They have washed their robes and made them white in the blood of the Lamb."

There they are. There *we* are—the multitude who so wanted to be faithful, who at times got defeated, soiled by life, and bested by trials, wearing the bloodied garments of life's tribulations, but through it all clung to the faith.

My friends, if this is not good news to you, you have never understood the gospel of grace.

Chapter Two

Magnificent Monotony

Sir James Jeans, the famous British astronomer, once said, "The universe appears to have been designed by a Pure Mathematician." Joseph Campbell wrote of "a perception of a cosmic order, mathematically definable." As they contemplated the order of the earth, the solar system, and the stellar universe, scientists and scholars have concluded that the Master Planner left nothing to chance.

The slant of the earth, for example, tilted at an angle of twenty-three degrees, produces our seasons. Scientists tell us that if the earth had not been tilted exactly as it is, vapors from the oceans would move both north and south, piling up vast continents of ice. —

If the moon were only 50,000 miles away from earth instead

of 250,000, the tides might be so enormous that all continents would be submerged in water—even the mountains would be eroded.

If the crust of the earth had been only ten feet thicker, there would be no oxygen, and without it all animal life would die.

Had the oceans been a few feet deeper, carbon dioxide and oxygen would have been absorbed and no vegetable life would exist.

The earth's weight has been estimated at six sextillion tons (that's a six with twenty-one zeros). Yet it is perfectly balanced and turns easily on its axis. It rotates daily at the rate of more than a thousand miles per hour, or 25,000 miles each day. This adds up to nine million miles a year. Considering the tremendous weight of six sextillion tons rolling at this fantastic speed around an invisible axis, held in place by unseen bands of gravitation, the words of Job 26:7 take on unparalleled significance: "He poised the earth on nothingness."

The earth revolves in its own orbit around the sun, making the long elliptical circuit of about six hundred million miles each year—which means we are traveling through space at nineteen miles per second or about 68,000 miles per hour.

Job further invites us to meditate on "the marvelous works of God" (37:14). Consider the sun. Every square yard of the sun's surface is emitting a constant energy level of 130,000 horsepower (that is, approximately 450 eight-cylinder automobile engines) in flames that are being produced by an energy source much more powerful than coal.

The nine major planets in our solar system range in distance from the sun from 36 million to about 3,664 million miles; yet

each moves around the sun in exact precision, with orbits rang-
ing from 88 days for Mercury to 248 years for Pluto.

Still, the sun is only one minor star among the 100 billion
burning orbs that comprise our Milky Way galaxy. If you were
to hold out a dime at arm's length while gazing at the night sky,
the coin would block out 15 million stars from your view, if
your eyes could see with that power.[1]

When we attempt to comprehend the almost countless stars
and other heavenly bodies in our galaxy alone, we resonate to
Isaiah's paean of praise to the all-powerful Creator: "Lift your eyes
and look: he who created these things leads out their army in
order, summoning each of them by name. So mighty is his power,
so great his strength, that not one fails to answer" (40:26).

Small wonder that David cries out:

Yahweh our Lord, how majestic is your name
throughout the world! Whoever keeps singing of your
majesty higher than the heavens, even through the
mouths of children, or of babes in arms, you make
him a fortress, firm against your foes, to subdue the
enemy and the rebel. I look up at your heavens,
shaped by your fingers, at the moon and the stars you
set firm, what are human beings that you spare a
thought for them, or the child of Adam that you care
for him? (Psalm 8)

Creation discloses a power that baffles our minds and
beggars our speech. We are enamored and enchanted by
God's power. We stutter and stammer about God's holiness.

We tremble before God's majesty…and yet we grow squeamish and skittish before God's love.

I am flabbergasted by the widespread refusal across this land to think big about a loving God. Like nervous thoroughbreds being guided to the starting gate at Churchill Downs, many Christians bray, bridle, and bolt at the revelation of God's all-embracing love in Jesus Christ.

In my ministry as a vagabond evangelist, I have encountered shocking resistance to the God whom the Bible defines as Love. The skeptics range from the oily, over-polite professionals who discreetly drop hints of the heresy of universalism, to the Bible thumper who sees only the dusty, robust war God of the Pentateuch, and who insists on restating the cold demands of rule-ridden perfectionism.

Our resistance to the furious love of God may be traced to the church, our parents and pastors, and life itself. They have hidden the face of a compassionate God, we protest, and favored a God of holiness, justice, and wrath.

Yet if we were truly men and women of prayer, our faces set like flint and our hearts laid waste by passion, we would discard our excuses. We would be done with blaming others.

We must go out into a desert of some kind (your backyard will do) and come into a personal experience of the awesome love of God. Then we will nod in knowing agreement with that gifted English mystic Julian of Norwich, "The greatest honor we can give Almighty God is to live gladly because of the knowledge of his love." We shall understand why, as Kittel's *Theological Dictionary of the New Testament* notes, that in the last years of his life on the island of Patmos, the apostle John wrote, and wrote with *magnificent monotony,* of the love of Jesus Christ. As if for the first time, we shall grasp what Paul meant when he said, "But however much sin increased, grace was always greater; so that as sin's reign brought death, so grace was to rule through saving justice that leads to eternal life through Jesus Christ our Lord" (Romans 5:20–21).

Just as John in the twilight of his life wrote largely of the love of Jesus, so Paul wrote lavishly of the gospel of grace:

- The grace of God is the totality by which men and women are made righteous (see Romans 3:24; Titus 3:7).
- By grace Paul was called (see Galatians 1:15).
- God bestows His glorious grace on us in His Son (see Ephesians 1:6).
- The grace of God appeared for the salvation of all (see Titus 2:11).
- The grace of our Lord has overflowed with the faith and love which are in Christ Jesus (see 1 Timothy 1:14).
- Grace is a store to which we have access through Christ (see Romans 5:2).
- Grace is a state or condition in which we stand (see Romans 5:2).
- It is received in abundance (see Romans 5:17).
- The grace of God has abounded more than sin (see Romans 5:15, 20–21; 6:1).
- Grace is given us in Christ (see 1 Corinthians 1:4).
- Paul did not receive it in vain (see 2 Corinthians 6:1).

- The surpassing grace of God is within the Christian (see 2 Corinthians 9:14).
- It extends to more and more people (see 2 Corinthians 4:15).
- Grace stands in opposition to works, which lack the power to save; if works had the power, the reality of grace would be annulled (see Romans 11:5ff; Ephesians 2:5, 7ff; 2 Timothy 1:9).
- Grace stands in opposition to the law. Both Jews and Gentiles are saved through the grace of the Lord Jesus (see Acts 15:11).
- To hold to the law is to nullify grace (see Galatians 2:21); and when the Galatians accept the law, they have fallen from grace (see Galatians 5:4).
- The Christian is not under the law but under grace (see Romans 6:14ff).
- Grace is opposed to what is owed (see Romans 4:4).
- The gospel itself, which is the good news of grace, can be called grace (see Acts 20:24) or the word of His grace (see Acts 14:3; 20:32).

Yes, the gracious God enfleshed in Jesus Christ *loves us.* Grace is the active expression of his love. The Christian lives by grace as Abba's child, utterly rejecting the God who catches people by surprise in a moment of weakness—the God incapable of smiling at our awkward mistakes, the God who does not accept a seat at our human festivities, the God who says "You will pay for that," the God incapable of understanding that children will always get dirty and be forgetful, the God always snooping around after sinners.

At the same time, the child of the Father rejects the pastel-colored patsy God who promises never to rain on our parade.

A pastor I know recalls a Sunday morning Bible study at his church when the text under consideration was Genesis 22. In this passage, God commands Abraham to take his son Isaac and offer him in sacrifice on Mount Moriah. After the group read the passage, the pastor offered some historical background on this period in salvation history, including the prevalence of child sacrifice among the Canaanites. The group listened in awkward silence.

Then the pastor asked, "But what does this story mean to *us*?"

A middle-aged man spoke up. "I'll tell you the meaning this story has for me. I've decided that me and my family are looking for another church."

The pastor was astonished, "What? Why?"

"Because," the man said, "when I look at that God, the God of Abraham, I feel I'm near a real God, not the sort of dignified, businesslike, Rotary Club God we chatter about here on Sunday mornings. Abraham's God could blow a man to bits, give and then take a child, ask for everything from a person, and then want more. I want to know *that* God."

The child of God knows that the graced life calls him or her to live on a cold and windy mountain, not on the flattened plain of reasonable, middle-of-the-road religion.

For at the heart of the gospel of grace, the sky darkens, the wind howls, a young man walks up another Moriah in obedience to a God who demands everything and stops at nothing.

Unlike Abraham, he carries a cross on his back rather than sticks for the fire…like Abraham, listening to a wild and restless God who will have His way with us, no matter what the cost.

This is the God of the gospel of grace. A God who, out of love for us, sent the only Son He ever had wrapped in our skin. He learned how to walk, stumbled and fell, cried for His milk, sweated blood in the night, was lashed with a whip and showered with spit, was fixed to a cross, and died whispering forgiveness on us all.

The God of the legalistic Christian, on the other hand, is often unpredictable, erratic, and capable of all manner of prejudices. When we view God this way, we feel compelled to engage in some sort of magic to appease Him. Sunday worship becomes a superstitious insurance policy against His whims. This God expects people to be perfect and to be in perpetual control of their feelings and thoughts. When broken people with this concept of God fail—as inevitably they must—they usually expect punishment. So they persevere in religious practices as they struggle to maintain a hollow image of a perfect self. The struggle itself is exhausting. The legalists can never live up to the expectations they project on God.

A married woman in Atlanta with two small children told me recently she was certain that God was disappointed with her because she wasn't "doing anything" for Him. She told me she felt called to a soup kitchen ministry but struggled with leaving her children in someone else's care. She was shocked when I told her the call was not from God but from her own ingrained legalism. Being a good mother wasn't enough for her; in her mind, neither was it good enough for God.

In similar fashion, a person who thinks of God as a loose cannon firing random broadsides to let us know who's in charge will become fearful, slavish, and probably unbending in his or her expectations of others. If your God is an impersonal cosmic force, your religion will be noncommittal and vague. The image of God as an omnipotent thug who brooks no human intervention creates a rigid lifestyle ruled by puritanical laws and dominated by fear.

But trust in the God who loves consistently and faithfully nurtures confident, free disciples. A loving God fosters a loving people. "The fact that our view of God shapes our lives to a great extent may be one of the reasons Scripture ascribes such importance to seeking to know Him."[2]

This truth is illustrated in the prophet Jonah's view of God. Jonah is so outraged when the Ninevites repent after his preaching that he wants to die. He didn't want God to forgive Nineveh; he wanted judgment. His narrow nationalism made it impossible for him to grasp the all-embracing love of God.[3] But the message of this prophetic book transcends the limits of the prophet. It proclaims how good God is, how His compassion extends to every creature in His universe, even (as the last word in the book says) "to the animals." All men and women are the people of His caring. All are called to accept the extravagant gift of His grace, for acceptance means simply to turn to God.

Jonah could not handle that. He lost his cool, grew livid when a castor-oil plant that was his sunscreen withered, yet he could let thousands of people perish in their unbelief without turning pale. Not a *bad* guy. After all, he was willing to give up the ghost for pagan sailors. Not bad; just myopic. God was *his*

God, the God of the Hebrews, imprisoned in one country, one temple, one ark of the covenant.

The theology of this sacred book is a clarion call to Israelites of both covenants: Think big about God. God's mercy on repentant Nineveh, on Jonah in his self-pity, even on brute animals, prepares the way for the gospel of grace. God is love.

> Over the years I've seen Christians shaping God in their own image—in each case a dreadfully small God. Some Roman Catholics still believe only they will graze heaven's green pastures... There is the God who has a special affection for capitalist America, regards the workaholic, and the God who loves only the poor and the underprivileged. There is a God who marches with victorious armies, and the God who loves only the meek who turns the other cheek. Some, like the elder brother in Luke, sulk and pout when the Father rocks and rolls, serves surf-and-turf for a prodigal son who has spent his last cent on whores. Some, tragically, refuse to believe that God can or will forgive them: *My sin is too great.*[4]

• This is not the God of grace who "wants everyone to be saved" (1 Timothy 2:4). This is not the God embodied in Jesus that Matthew came to know. This is not the God who calls sinners—which, as you and I know, means everybody.

I am reminded of a marvelous scene in Flannery O'Connor's short story "Revelation," based on the last book of the Bible. The main character is Mrs. Turpin, a self-righteous woman, proud of her good disposition, good deeds, and sense of decency. She has low regard for blacks and white trash. She hates freaks and the mentally ill. *X was more tet+X*

Well, one day Mrs. Turpin goes to the doctor's office and finds herself surrounded by the people she despises. Suddenly a young woman with acne strides across the room, hits Mrs. Turpin with a book, and tries to strangle her. When order is finally restored, Mrs. Turpin, like she was awaiting a revelation, asks, "What you got to say to me?"

And the young girl shouts, "Go back to hell where you came from, you old wart hog!"

Mrs. Turpin is shattered. Her world has collapsed. The God she had fashioned in her own image, so <u>pleased with her piety, has vanished.</u>

She goes home and stands in her backyard, staring at the pigpen. And she receives a vision. From the ground a brilliant, swinging, fiery bridge is raised from earth to heaven and along that bridge "a vast horde of souls were rumbling toward heaven. There were whole companies of white trash, clean for the first time in their lives, and bands of blacks in white robes, and battalions of <u>freaks</u> and <u>lunatics</u> shouting and clapping and leaping like frogs," and finally a whole tribe of people just like herself "marching behind the others with great dignity, accountable as they had always been for good order and common sense and respectable behavior. They alone were on key. Yet she could see by their shocked and altered faces that even <u>their virtues were being burned away."</u> *What should we burn away?*

The story ends with Mrs. Turpin going back into her house, hearing only "the voices of the souls climbing upward into the starry field and shouting hallelujah."[5]

Perhaps a touch of Mrs. Turpin hides in a lot of holy people. A friend of mine once told me years ago that the one thing that made her uneasy about heaven is that she won't get to choose her table companions at the Messianic banquet. — ???

Our experience of God's unconditional love must be shaped by the Scriptures. God's written Word must take hold of us as His spoken Word took hold of Isaiah and Jeremiah, Ezekiel and Hosea; as the spoken Word of Christ mesmerized Matthew and Mary Magdalene and captivated Simon Peter and the Samaritan woman.

The Word we study has to be the Word we pray. My personal experience of the relentless tenderness of God came not from exegetes, theologians, and spiritual writers, but from sitting still in the presence of the living Word and beseeching Him to help me understand with my head and heart His written Word. Sheer scholarship alone cannot reveal to us the gospel of grace. We must never allow the authority of books, institutions, or leaders to replace the authority of *knowing* Jesus Christ personally and directly. When the religious views of others interpose between us and the primary experience of Jesus as the Christ, we become unconvicted and unpersuasive travel agents handing out brochures to places we have never visited.

In his famous 1522 Christmas sermon, Martin Luther cried out:

O that God should desire that my interpretation and that of all teachers should disappear, and each Christian should come straight to the Scripture alone and to the pure word of God! You see from this babbling of mine the immeasurable difference between the word of God and all human words, and how no man can adequately reach and explain a single word of God with all his words. It is an eternal word and must be understood and contemplated with a quiet mind. No one else can understand except a mind that contemplates in silence. For anyone who could achieve this without commentary or interpretation, my commentaries and those of everyone else could not only be of no use, but merely a hindrance. Go to the Bible itself, dear Christians, and let my expositions and those of all scholars be no more than a tool with which to build aright, so that we can understand, taste, and abide in the simple and pure word of God; for God dwells alone in Zion.[6] — PREACH

Philosopher Jacques Maritain once said that the culmination of knowledge is not conceptual but experiential—I feel God. Such is the promise of the Scriptures: "Be still and acknowledge [experience] that I am God" (Psalm 46:10). My own journey bears witness to that. I mean simply that a living, loving God can and does make His presence felt, can and does speak to us in the silence of our hearts, can and does warm and caress us till we no longer doubt that He is near, that He is here. Such experience is pure grace to the poor, the children and the sinners, the privileged types in the gospel of grace. It cannot be forced from God. He gives it freely, but He does give it and has given it to such as Moses and Matthew and me. In fact, there is no one to whom God denies it. Ignatius of Loyola said, "The direct experience of God is grace indeed, and basically there is no one to whom it is refused."

In essence, there is only one thing God asks of us—that we be men and women of prayer, people who live close to God, people for whom God is everything and for whom God is enough. That is the root of peace. We have that peace when the gracious God is all we seek. When we start seeking something besides Him, we lose it. As Merton said in the last public address before his death, "That is his call to us—simply to be people who are content to live close to him and to renew the kind of life in which the closeness is felt and experienced."

There was a time in my life when I knew nothing of this gracious God and His gospel of grace. Prior to my encounter with Jesus, my personal life was riddled with guilt, shame, fear, self-hatred, and obviously, low self-esteem. You see, growing up Catholic from the late 1930s through the 1950s, my central preoccupation was sin. Sin was everywhere; it consumed us and dominated our consciousness.

There were two kinds of sin: *mortal*, which was the more serious kind, and *venial*. Committing a mortal sin means knowing that what you are about to do, think, want, or say is really bad…but doing, thinking, wanting, or saying it anyway. Most of the things we did wrong fell into the less offensive category of venial sin. Committing a venial sin meant doing something that is not really so bad, or doing something really bad that you don't *think* is really bad or that your heart really isn't into doing. If your little brother is being a pest and you tell him to drop dead, you've committed a venial sin. If you shoot him dead, you've committed a mortal sin.

While the difference between mortal and venial sin seems

obvious, don't be fooled. There is more to this than meets the eye. What is really bad and what isn't? And who decides?

Here is a routine situation that every Catholic of my generation had to deal with: You are at a baseball game at Yankee Stadium on a Friday night in June 1950. Catholics are forbidden to eat meat under penalty of mortal sin. But you want a hot dog. Now, just considering eating meat on Friday is a venial sin; wanting to is another. You have not moved in your seat and you have already sinned twice.

What if you actually ate one? Aside from the risk of choking on forbidden food and getting punished right on the spot, have you committed a mortal sin or a venial sin? Well, if you think it's mortal, it may be mortal; and if you think it's venial, it still may be mortal. After much thought, you decide it's venial. You call the hot dog vendor, you take the money out of your pocket, and you buy a hot dog. This is clearly an act of free will. You figure you can go confess your sin to the priest on Saturday night. But wait! Does a venial sin become mortal when you commit it deliberately? That's a chance you take. What if you've forgotten it's Friday? In that case, eating the hot dog may not be a sin, but forgetting it's Friday is. What if you remember it's Friday halfway through the hot dog? Is it a venial sin to finish it? If you throw it away, is wasting food a sin? Within five minutes you have committed enough sins to land you in purgatory for a million years. The simplest thing to do is not to take any chances—stay away from Yankee Stadium on Fridays.

Being a Catholic in those days meant a lifelong struggle to avoid sin, mortal or venial. While you didn't want to go to hell, you didn't want to rot in purgatory either. So you played it safe:

Think about every thought, word, action, desire, and omission, and figure that everything you want to do is a sin.[7]

In retrospect, while much of this stuff is hilarious, the sense of guilt and shame were terribly real. On a warm summer night in June 1947, I reached puberty and my curiosity got the best of me. Panicked, I raced to the local church, and confessed a sin common to many a young man. The priest thundered in response, "You did what?! Do you know you could go to hell for that?" His voice boomed through the crowded church. I went home humiliated and frightened. (Since then, I have met many gentle, wise, and compassionate confessors, and the warm winds of spring are blowing through the Catholic church after a long, cold winter.)

Over the years, the growing consciousness of radical grace has wrought profound changes in my self-awareness. Justification by grace through faith means that I know myself accepted by God as I am. When my head is enlightened and my heart is pierced by this truth, I can accept myself *as I am*. Genuine self-acceptance is not derived from the power of positive thinking, mind games, or pop psychology. *It is an act of faith* in the God of grace.

Several times in my ministry people have expressed the fear that self-acceptance will abort the ongoing conversion process and lead to a life of spiritual laziness and moral laxity. Nothing could be more untrue. The acceptance of self does not mean to be resigned to the status quo. On the contrary, the more fully we accept ourselves, the more successfully we begin to grow. Love is a far better stimulus than threat or pressure.

One saint used to say that she was the type of woman who advances more rapidly when she is drawn by love than when driven by fear. She was perceptive enough to know that we are all that type of person. It is possible to attain great holiness of life while still being prone to pettiness and insincerity, sensuality and envy, but the first move will always be to recognize that I am that way. In terms of spiritual growth the faith-conviction that God accepts me as I am is a tremendous help to become better.[8]

we are all this way

When we accept ourselves for what we are, we decrease our hunger for power or the acceptance of others because our self-intimacy reinforces our inner sense of security. We are no longer preoccupied with being powerful or popular. We no longer fear criticism because we accept the reality of our human limitations. Once integrated, we are less often plagued with the desire to please others because simply being true to ourselves brings lasting peace. We are grateful for life and we deeply appreciate and love ourselves.

This chapter began with a paean of praise of the power of God manifested in the works of creation. The gospel of grace ends any apparent dichotomy between God's power and His love. For the work of creating is an act of love. The God who flung from His fingertips this universe filled with galaxies and stars, penguins and puffins, gulls and gannets, Pomeranians and poodles, elephants and evergreens, parrots and potato bugs, peaches and pears, and a world full of children made in His own image, is the God who loves with magnificent monotony.

And anyone who has experienced the love of the Lord of the Dance will tell you: The synonym for monotonous is not *boring*.

Chapter Three

THE RAGAMUFFIN GOSPEL

*A*fter reading the entire Gospel of Luke for the first time, a post-Valley girl said: "Wow! Like Jesus has this totally intense thing for ragamuffins."

The young lady is onto something.

Jesus spent a disproportionate amount of time with people described in the Gospels as the poor, the blind, the lame, the lepers, the hungry, sinners, prostitutes, tax collectors, the persecuted, the downtrodden, the captives, those possessed by unclean spirits, all who labor and are heavy burdened, the rabble who know nothing of the law, the crowds, the little ones, the least, the last, and the lost sheep of the house of Israel.

In short, Jesus hung out with ragamuffins.

Obviously His love for failures and nobodies was not an exclusive love—that would merely substitute one class prejudice for another. He related with warmth and compassion to the middle and upper classes not because of their family connections, financial clout, intelligence, or Social Register status, but because they, too, were God's children. While the term *poor* in the gospel includes the economically deprived and embraces all the oppressed who are dependent upon the mercy of others, it extends to all who rely entirely upon the mercy of God and accept the gospel of grace—the poor in spirit (Matthew 5:3).

Jesus' preference for little people and partiality toward ragamuffins is an irrefutable fact of the gospel narrative. As the French philosopher Maurice Blondel said, "If you really want to understand a man, don't just listen to what he says but watch what he does."

One of the mysteries of the gospel tradition is this strange attraction of Jesus for the unattractive, this strange desire for the undesirable, this strange love for the unlovely. The key to this mystery is, of course, Abba. Jesus does what He sees the Father doing; He loves those whom the Father loves.[1]

In His reply to the disciples' question about who is the greatest in the kingdom of heaven (Matthew 18), Jesus abolished any distinction between the elite and the ordinary in the Christian community.

So he called a little child to him whom he set among them. Then he said, "In truth I tell you, unless you change and become like little children you will never enter the kingdom of Heaven. And so, the one who makes himself as little as this little child is the greatest in the kingdom of Heaven." (vv. 2–4)

Jesus cuts to the heart of the matter as He sets the child on His knee. The child is unself-conscious, incapable of pretense. I am reminded of the night little John Dyer, three years old, knocked on our door flanked by his parents. I looked down and said, "Hi, John. I am delighted to see you." He looked neither to the right nor left. His face was set like flint. He narrowed his eyes with the apocalyptic glint of an aimed gun. "Where's the cookies?" he demanded.

The kingdom belongs to people who aren't trying to look good or impress anybody, even themselves. They are not plotting how they can call attention to themselves, worrying about how their actions will be interpreted or wondering if they will get gold stars for their behavior. Twenty centuries later, Jesus speaks pointedly to the preening ascetic trapped in the fatal narcissism of spiritual perfectionism, to those of us caught up in boasting about our victories in the vineyard, to those of us fretting and flapping about our human weaknesses and character defects. The child doesn't have to struggle to get himself in a good position for having a relationship with God; he doesn't have to craft ingenious ways of explaining his position to Jesus; he doesn't have to create a pretty face for himself; he doesn't have to achieve any state of spiritual feeling or intellectual understanding. All he has to do is happily accept the cookies: the gift of the kingdom.

When Jesus tells us to become like little children, He is inviting us to forget what lies behind. Little John Dyer has no past. Whatever we have done in the past, be it good or evil, great or small, is irrelevant to our stance before God today. It is only *now* that we are in the presence of God.

The meaning of living in fidelity to the present moment, neither retreating to the past nor anticipating the future, is wonderfully illustrated by a Zen story about a monk being pursued by a ferocious tiger. The monk raced to the edge of a cliff, glanced back, and saw the growling tiger about to spring. The monk spotted a rope dangling over the edge of the cliff. He grabbed it and began shinnying down the side of the cliff out of the clutches of the tiger. *Whew!* Narrow escape. The monk then looked down and saw a quarry of jagged rocks five hundred feet below. He looked up and saw the tiger poised atop the cliff with bared claws. Just then, two mice began to nibble at the rope. What to do?

The monk saw a strawberry within arm's reach, growing out of the face of the cliff. He plucked it, ate it, and exclaimed, "Yum! That's the best strawberry I've ever tasted in my entire life." If he had been preoccupied with the rock below (the future) or the tiger above (the past), he would have missed the strawberry God was giving him in the present moment. Children do not focus on the tigers of the past or the future but only on the strawberry that comes *in the here and now.*

The apostle Paul grasped the full meaning of Jesus' teaching on becoming like a little child. Serving as a coatrack during the stoning of Stephen and as a ringleader in the slaughter of Christians, Paul might well have become pathological had he dwelt on his pre-Christian past. But he writes, "I can only say that forgetting all that lies behind me, and straining forward to what lies in front" (Philippians 3:13).

Whatever past achievements might bring us honor, whatever past disgraces might make us blush, all have been crucified with Christ and exist no more except in the deep recesses of eternity, where "good is enhanced into glory and evil miraculously established as part of the greater good."[2]

It is important to remember the Jewish attitude toward children in first-century Palestine if we are to grasp the full force of Jesus' teaching here. In the present day, we tend to idealize childhood as the happy age of innocence, insouciance, and simple faith; but in New Testament times the child was considered of no importance, meriting little attention or favor. "Children in that society had no status at all—they did not count."[3] The child was regarded with scorn.

For the disciple of Jesus, "becoming like a little child" means the willingness to accept oneself as being of little account and to be regarded as unimportant. The little child who is the image of the kingdom is a symbol of those who have the lowest places in society, the poor and the oppressed, the beggars, the prostitutes and tax collectors—the people whom Jesus often called the "little ones" or the "least." Jesus' concern was that these little ones should not be despised or treated as inferior (see Matthew 18:10). He was well aware of their feelings of shame and inferiority, and because of His compassion they were, in His eyes, of extraordinarily great value. As far as He was concerned, they had nothing to fear. The kingdom was theirs. "There is no need to be afraid, little flock, for it has pleased your Father to give you the kingdom" (Luke 12:32).

Jesus gave these scorned little ones a privileged place in the kingdom and presented them as models to would-be disciples. They were to accept the kingdom in the same way a child would accept her allowance. If the children were privileged, it was not because they had merited privilege, but simply because God took pleasure in these little ones whom adults despised. The mercy of Jesus flowed out to them wholly from unmerited grace and divine preference.

The hymn of jubilation in Luke carries the same theme: "I bless you, Father, Lord of heaven and earth, for hiding these things from the wise and clever and revealing them to mere children. Yes, Father, for that is what it pleased you to do."

The scribes were treated with excessive deference in Jewish society because of their education and learning. Everyone honored them because of their wisdom and intelligence. The "mere children" (*napioi* in Greek, really meaning babes) were Jesus' image for the uneducated and ignorant.[4] He is saying that the gospel of grace has been disclosed to and grasped by the uneducated and ignorant instead of the learned and wise. For this, Jesus thanks God.

The babes *(napioi)* are in the same state as the children *(paidia)*. God's grace falls on them because they are negligible creatures, not because of their good qualities. They may be aware of their worthlessness, but this is not the reason revelations are given to them. Jesus expressly attributes their good fortune to the Father's good pleasure, the divine *eudokia.* The gifts are not determined by the slightest personal quality or virtue. They were pure liberality. Once and for all, Jesus deals the death blow to any distinction between the elite and the ordinary in the Christian community.

Further light is cast on the ragamuffin gospel by the sinner's privilege. As I mentioned earlier, Jesus is seated at a table in Levi's house when the scribes and Pharisees badger Him as to why He consorts with ragamuffins. Jesus says to them, "I have come to call sinners, not the self-righteous."

The sinners to whom Jesus directed His messianic ministry were not those who skipped morning devotions or Sunday church. His ministry was to those whom society considered *real* sinners. They had done nothing to merit salvation. Yet they opened themselves to the gift that was offered them. On the other hand, the self-righteous placed their trust in the works of the Law and closed their hearts to the message of grace.

But the salvation Jesus brought could not be earned. There could be no bargaining with God in a petty poker table atmosphere: "I have done this; therefore you owe me that." Jesus utterly destroys the juridical notion that our works demand payment in return. Our puny works do not entitle us to barter with God. Everything depends upon His good pleasure.

Several years ago I remember an angry letter written to the editor of a national evangelical magazine by an irate Catholic priest actively involved in the ministry of evangelism. He vehemently protested the cover story and picture of Francis MacNutt, also a Catholic priest with a worldwide healing ministry. MacNutt had recently married. The letter writer demanded to know why a previous article done on himself had been buried in the back of the magazine without a photo. He had stayed celibate all these years and had been given second-class treatment, while MacNutt, who had disobeyed the Pope and resigned the priesthood, was given star status. The author of the letter deemed the whole thing grossly unfair.

My wife, Roslyn, read his letter and remarked, "Shades of the elder brother of the prodigal son!"

However, this decided uneasiness with the ragamuffin gospel is not confined to one Christian tradition. In every denomination and nondenominational persuasion Christians are seeking to win God's favor by plunging into more spiritual activities, multiplying altars and sacrifices, making charitable contributions, lengthening the time of formal prayer, and getting involved in more church-related organizations.

There is need for careful discernment here. The evidence of earnestness, sincerity, and effort is considerable. The Christian's lifestyle is pious, proper, and correct. What's missing?

He or she has not surrendered to the Christ of grace.

The danger with our good works, spiritual investments, and all the rest of it is that we can construct a picture of ourselves in which we situate our self-worth. Complacency then replaces sheer delight in God's unconditional love. Our doing becomes the very undoing of the ragamuffin gospel.

Nowhere in the New Testament is the privileged position of turkeys, nobodies, and marginal people on the fringes of society disclosed more dramatically than in Jesus' ministry of meal sharing.

In modern times it is scarcely possible to appreciate the scandal Jesus caused by His table fellowship with sinners.

In the year 1925, if a wealthy plantation owner in Atlanta extended a formal invitation to four colored cotton pickers to come to his mansion for Sunday dinner, preceded by cocktails and followed by several hours of brandy and conversation, the Georgia aristocracy would have been outraged, neighboring Alabama infuriated, and the Ku Klux Klan apoplectic. Sixty or seventy years ago in the deep South, the caste system was inviolable, social and racial discrimination inflexible, and indiscretion made the loss of reputation inevitable.[5]

In first-century Palestinian Judaism the class system was enforced rigorously. It was legally forbidden to mingle with sinners who were outside the law: table fellowship with beggars, tax collectors (traitors to the national cause because they were collecting taxes *for* Rome from their own people to get a kickback from the take), and prostitutes was religiously, socially, and culturally taboo.

Sadly, the meaning of meal sharing is largely lost in the Christian community today. In the Near East, to share a meal with someone is a guarantee of peace, trust, fraternity, and forgiveness—the shared table symbolizes a shared life. An Orthodox Jew's saying "I would like to have dinner with you" is a metaphor that implies, "I would like to enter into friendship with you." Even today an American Jew will share a doughnut and a cup of coffee with you, but to extend a dinner invitation is to say, "Come to my *mikdash me-at,* the miniature sanctuary of my dining room table, where we will celebrate the

most sacred and beautiful experience that life affords—
friendship." That is what Zacchaeus heard when Jesus called
him down from the sycamore tree, and that is why Jesus' practice of table fellowship caused hostile comment from the outset
of His ministry.

It did not escape the Pharisees' attention that Jesus meant to
befriend the rabble. He was not only breaking the law, He was
destroying the very structure of Jewish society. "They all complained when they saw what was happening. 'He has gone to
stay at a sinner's house,' they said" (Luke 19:7). But Zacchaeus,
not too hung up on respectability, was overwhelmed with joy.

> It would be impossible to overestimate the impact
> these meals must have had upon the poor and the
> sinners. By accepting them as friends and equals Jesus
> had taken away their shame, humiliation, and guilt.
> By showing them that they mattered to him as people
> he gave them a sense of dignity and released them
> from their old captivity. The physical contact which
> he must have had with them at table (see John 13:25)
> and which he obviously never dreamed of disallowing
> (see Luke 7:38–39) must have made them feel clean
> and acceptable. Moreover, because Jesus was looked
> upon as a man of God and a prophet, they would
> have interpreted his gesture of friendship as God's
> approval on them. They were now acceptable to God.
> Their sinfulness, ignorance, and uncleanness had
> been overlooked and were no longer being held
> against them.[6]

Through table fellowship Jesus ritually acted out His insight into Abba's indiscriminate love—a love that causes His sun to rise on bad men as well as good, and His rain to fall on honest and dishonest men alike (see Matthew 5:45). The inclusion of sinners in the community of salvation, symbolized in table fellowship, is the most dramatic expression of the ragamuffin gospel and the merciful love of the redeeming God.

Thorough biblical research indicates that Jesus either had His own home in Capernaum or at least shared one with Peter, Andrew, and their families. Undoubtedly, in His ministry as an itinerant evangelist, Jesus often slept on the side of the road or stayed with friends: "The Son of man has nowhere to lay his head" (Matthew 8:20). But we may have taken this statement too literally. "It is difficult to understand how Jesus could have been accused of entertaining sinners (see Luke 15:2) if he did not have some kind of home in which to do so."[7]

Upon returning home from His missionary journeys, Jesus probably had some kind of quasi-permanent residence wherein He often served as host. Meal sharing occurred with such regularity that Jesus was accused of being a drunkard and a glutton (see Luke 7:34). The guest list would include a ragtag parade of donkey peddlers, prostitutes, herdsmen, slumlords, and gamblers. A social climber Jesus was not.

Status seekers today are selective about their dinner guests and make elaborate preparations (linen, china, silver, fresh flowers, an exquisite Beaujolais, truffle sauce, Long Island duck with glazed raspberries, Death by Chocolate dessert, and so on) for people they want to stand well with. Then they anxiously await the morning mail to see if their dinner invitation is reciprocated.

Consciously or unconsciously, the social gadflies of our day do not underestimate the ritual power of meal sharing. Jesus' sinner guests were well aware that table fellowship entailed more than mere politeness or courtesy. It meant peace, acceptance, reconciliation, and brotherhood. "For Jesus this fellowship at table with those whom the devout had written off was not merely the expression of liberal tolerance and humanitarian sentiment. It was the expression of his mission and message: peace and reconciliation for all, without exception, even for the moral failures."8

The gospel portrait of Jesus is that of a person who cherished life and especially other people as loving gifts from the Father's hand. The peripheral figures whom Jesus encountered in His ministry reacted in various ways to His person and His message, but few responded with gloom or sadness. (And they were those, such as the rich young ruler, who rejected His message.) The living presence of Jesus awakened joy and set people free. Joy was in fact the most characteristic result of all His ministry to ragamuffins.

John's disciples and the Pharisees were keeping a fast, when some people came to him and said to him, "Why is it that John's disciples and the disciples of the Pharisees fast, but your disciples do not?" Jesus replied, "Surely the bridegroom's attendants cannot fast while the bridegroom is still with them? As long as they have the bridegroom with them, they cannot fast." (Mark 2:18–19)

Jesus feasted while John fasted. Whereas John's call to conversion was essentially linked to penitential practices, the call of

Jesus is fundamentally connected to being a table companion, eating and drinking with Jesus in whom God's merciful manner with sinners is manifested. Breaking bread with Jesus was a festive celebration of good fellowship in which there was salvation. Asceticism was not only inappropriate but unthinkable in the presence of the Bridegroom.

This remarkable passage illuminates the extraordinary enchantment cast by the Carpenter-Messiah. The ragamuffins discovered that sharing a meal with Him was a liberating experience of sheer joy. He freed them from self-hatred, exhorted them not to confuse their perception of themselves with the mystery they really were, gave them what they needed more than anything else—encouragement for their lives—and delivered reassuring words such as "Do not live in fear, little flock; don't be afraid; fear is useless, what is needed is trust; stop worrying; cheer up—your sins are all forgiven." Small wonder that the evangelist Mark preserved this memory of Jesus with the utmost care.

The contagious joy of Jesus (only carriers can pass it on) infected and freed His followers. The author of Hebrews says, "Jesus Christ is the same today as he was yesterday and as he will be for ever" (13:8). If Jesus appeared at your dining room table tonight with knowledge of everything you are and are not, total comprehension of your life story and every skeleton hidden in your closet; if He laid out the real state of your present discipleship with the hidden agenda, the mixed motives, and the dark desires buried in your psyche, you would feel His acceptance and forgiveness. For "experiencing God's love in Jesus Christ means experiencing that one has been unreservedly accepted, approved and infinitely loved, that one can and should accept oneself and one's neighbor. Salvation is joy in God which expresses itself in joy in and with one's neighbor."[9]

Therefore, it is unimaginable to picture a wooden-faced, stoic, joyless, and judgmental Jesus as He reclined with ragamuffins. The human personality of Jesus is underrated when it is perceived as a passive mask for the dramatic speeches of divinity. Such timidity robs Jesus of His humanity, encases Him in plaster of paris, and concludes that He neither laughed, cried, smiled, nor got hurt, but simply passed through our world without emotional engagement.

Mark records that a group of parents, who obviously sensed something of God's love in Jesus, wanted Him to bless their little ones. The irritated disciples, fatigued by the long day's journey on foot from Capernaum to the district of Judea and the far side of the Jordan, attempted to shoo away the children. Jesus became visibly upset and silenced the Twelve with a withering glance. Mark notes carefully that Jesus picked them up *one by one*, cradled them, and gave each of them His blessing.

My friend Robert Frost comments:

I am so glad Jesus didn't suggest they group all the children together for a sort of general blessing because he was tired. Instead he took time to hold each child close to his heart and to earnestly pray for them all…then they joyfully scampered off to bed. One is tenderly reminded of a beautiful messianic passage from the prophets. "He will feed his flock like a shepherd, he will gather the lambs in his arms, he will carry them in his

bosom, and will gently lead those that have their young"
(Isaiah 40:11). I think there is a lesson here for anyone
who would seek to set any kind of false condition con-
cerning *just who should be the recipients of God's grace.*
He blessed them all.[10]

A brief digression: There is a wondrous open-mindedness
about children and an insatiable desire to learn from life. An
open attitude is like an open door—a welcoming disposition
toward the fellow travelers who knock on our door during the
middle of a day, the middle of the week, or the middle of a lifetime. Some are dirtballs, grungy, disheveled, and bedraggled.
The sophisticated adult within me shudders and is reluctant to
offer them hospitality. They may be carrying precious gifts
under their shabby rags, but I still prefer clean-shaven
Christians who are neatly attired, properly pedigreed, and who
affirm my vision, echo my thoughts, stroke me, and make me
feel good. Yet my inner child protests, "I want new friends, not
old mirrors."

When our inner child is not nurtured and nourished, our
minds gradually close to new ideas, unprofitable commitments,
and the surprises of the Spirit. Evangelical faith is bartered for
cozy, comfortable piety. A failure of nerve and an unwillingness
to risk distorts God into a Bookkeeper, and the gospel of grace
is swapped for the security of religious bondage.

"Unless you become as little children…" Heaven will be
filled with five-year-olds.

Burkhardt writes, "I fear for the lawyer whose only life is
corporate tax, the doctor whose whole existence is someone

else's prostate, the business executive whose single responsibility is to his stockholders, the athlete who puts all his eggs in an 18-inch basket, the theologian who thinks the world can be saved by theology… A closed mind kills marriages and human relations; it deadens feelings and sensitivities; it makes for a church that lives in a thousand and one tunnels, with no communication and no exit."[11]

If we maintain the open-mindedness of children, we challenge fixed ideas and established structures, including our own. We listen to people in other denominations and religions. We don't find demons in those with whom we disagree. We don't cozy up to people who mouth our jargon. If we are open, we rarely resort to either/or—either creation or evolution, liberty or law, sacred or secular, Beethoven or Madonna. We focus on both/and, fully aware that God's truth cannot be imprisoned in a small definition. Of course, the open mind does not accept everything indiscriminately—Marxism and capitalism, Christianity and atheism, love and lust, Moët Chandon and vinegar. It does not absorb all propositions equally like a sponge, nor is it as soft. But the open mind realizes that reality, truth, and Jesus Christ are incredibly open-ended. (Digression foreclosed.)

The ragamuffin spirit of Jesus sometimes surfaces in the most unlikely settings and is often totally absent in places we most expect to find it. Let me close this chapter with a tale of two communities—both cut close to the bone of my existence: One concerns alcoholics, the other involves Roslyn.

On a sweltering summer night in New Orleans, sixteen recovering alcoholics and drug addicts gather for their weekly

AA meeting. Although several members attend other meetings during the week, this is their home group. They have been meeting on Tuesday nights for several years and know each other well. Some talk to each other daily on the telephone; others socialize outside the meetings. The personal investment in one another's sobriety is sizable. Nobody fools anybody else. Everyone is there because he or she made a slobbering mess of his or her life and is trying to put the pieces back together. Each meeting is marked by levity and seriousness. Some members are wealthy, others middle class or poor. Some smoke, others don't. Most drink coffee. Some have graduate degrees, others have not finished high school. For one small hour, the high and the mighty descend and the lowly rise. The result is fellowship.

The meeting opened with the Serenity Prayer followed by a moment of silence. The prologue to Alcoholics Anonymous was read from the Big Book by Harry, followed by the Twelve Steps of the program from Michelle. That night, Jack was the appointed leader. "The theme I would like to talk about tonight is gratitude," he began, "but if anyone wants to talk about something else, let's hear it."

Immediately Phil's hand shot up.

"As you all know, last week I went up to Pennsylvania to visit family and missed the meeting. You also know I have been sober for seven years. Last Monday I got drunk and stayed drunk for five days."

The only sound in the room was the drip of Mr. Coffee in the corner.

"You all know the buzz word, H.A.L.T., in this program," he continued. "Don't let yourself get hungry, angry, lonely, or tired or you will be very vulnerable for the first drink. The last three got to me. I unplugged the jug and…"

Phil's voice choked and he lowered his head. I glanced around the table—moist eyes, tears of compassion, soft sobbing the only sound in the room.

"The same thing happened to me, Phil, but I stayed drunk for a year."

"Thank God you're back."

"Boy, that took a lot of guts."

"Relapse spells relief, Phil," said a substance abuse counselor.

"Let's get together tomorrow and figure out what you needed relief from and why."

"I'm so proud of you."

"I never made even close to seven years."

As the meeting ended, Phil stood up. He felt a hand on his shoulder, another on his face. Then kisses on his eyes, forehead, neck, and cheek. "You old ragamuffin," said Denise. "Let's go. I'm treating you to a banana split at Tastee Freeze."

The second scenario occurred when Roslyn was taking a graduate course in religious education at Loyola University in New Orleans in the summer of 1981.

Dr. Meghan McKenna was lecturing on the New Testament milieu in which Jesus' ministry began. The four dominant religious groups were the Pharisees, Sadducees, Zealots, and Essenes. The Pharisees separated themselves from everyone who was not faithful to the law and the traditions, in order to form closed communities, the faithful remnant of Israel. Their name means "the separate ones"—i.e., the holy ones, the true community of Israel. Their morality was legalistic and bourgeois, a matter of reward and punishment: God loved and rewarded those who kept the law and hated and punished those who did not.

Dr. McKenna discussed the position of the Sadducees, mostly conservative and largely composed of the wealthy aristocracy; the Zealots, who viewed submission to Rome as an act of unfaithfulness to God; the Essenes, who rejected everyone who did not belong to their sect. They separated themselves completely from society and lived a celibate and ascetic life in the desert. All outsiders were to be hated as the sons of darkness. Love and respect were reserved for members of their group—the sons of light.

The "sinners," McKenna continued, were social outcasts. Anyone who for any reason deviated from the law and the customs of the middle class (the educated and virtuous, the Scribes and Pharisees) was treated as inferior, as low class. The sinners were a well-defined social group.

As her lecture ended, Dr. McKenna suggested, "Let's do a little exercise right here in the classroom. Would all those who do not smoke stand up, walk to the left and stand by the wall. And reformed smokers stand in the center of the room. Those who still smoke form a group on the right."

Thirty of the professionals had never smoked, twelve were reformed, and three were active smokers. "At that time," Roslyn says, "I belonged to the latter group. An immediate sense of separation was obvious."

"Let's discuss two questions," McKenna said. "First, how do you feel about the current smoking regulations on campus, in restaurants, airports, the corporate world, and so forth?"

All three groups unanimously agreed that the regulations were good, ecologically important, and sensitive to the health and welfare of others.

"The second question: How do you feel about smokers personally?"

"They are disgusting and inconsiderate," said one non-smoker.

"Obviously anyone who smokes has low self-esteem and a lousy self-image," voiced another.

"They have no willpower."

"Rotten role models for teenagers."

"I have serious questions about the quality of their faith and depth of their personal relationship with Christ."

"Don't they know they are poisoning the atmosphere?"

Roslyn says, "I cowered against the far wall, feeling like the woman caught in adultery. Suddenly the environment was so hostile. For the past four years of graduate school, I had prayed, worshiped, gone on picnics, taken coffee breaks, studied, and conversed with these people. I felt a deep sense of bonding because of our shared life and ministry. The reformed smokers were much more understanding because they had been there— the place of addiction. At first, I was angry. When the inner rage finally subsided, I wanted to weep. I have never felt so alone.

"The bell sounded and class ended. We filed out of the room in silence."

The next day Dr. McKenna, following her usual procedure, asked her students to share their feelings and reactions to the exercise of the previous day.

"Yesterday I learned something about myself," said the

woman who had made the harshest and most judgmental comments during the exercise. "I need a lot more compassion for people who are different from myself."

"How did you feel yesterday, Roslyn?" inquired the teacher.

"When I was standing against the wall, I actually thought the Group 1 people would have thrown stones at us were they available. I realized how difficult it was for me to look at them and say, 'Father, forgive them, for they know not what they do.'"

Dr. McKenna's exercise achieved what it set out to accomplish. The fierce words of Jesus addressed to the Pharisees of His day stretch across the bands of time. Today they are directed not only to fallen televangelists but to each of us. We miss Jesus' point entirely when we use His words as weapons against others. They are to be taken personally by each of us. This is the form and shape of Christian Pharisaism in our time. Hypocrisy is not the prerogative of people in high places. The most impoverished among us is capable of it. "Hypocrisy is the natural expression of what is meanest in us all."[12]

The ragamuffin gospel reveals that Jesus forgives sins, including sins of the flesh; that He is comfortable with sinners who remember how to show compassion; but that He cannot and will not have a relationship with pretenders in the Spirit.

Perhaps the real dichotomy in the Christian community today is not between conservatives and liberals or creationists and evolutionists but between the awake and the asleep. The Christian ragamuffin acknowledges with Macbeth, "Life's but a walking shadow, a poor player that struts and frets his hour upon the stage and then is heard no more."[13] Just as a smart man knows he is stupid, so the awake Christian knows that he/she is a ragamuffin.

Although truth is not always humility, humility is always truth—the blunt acknowledgment that I owe my life, being, and salvation to Another. This fundamental act lies at the core of our response to grace.

The beauty of the ragamuffin gospel lies in the insight it offers into Jesus: the essential tenderness of His heart, His way of looking at the world, His mode of relating to you and me. "If you really want to understand a man, don't just listen to what he says, but watch what he does."

Chapter Four

Tilted Halos

A man walked into the doctor's office and said, "Doctor, I have this awful headache that never leaves me. Could you give me something for it?"

"I will," said the doctor, "but I want to check a few things out first. Tell me, do you drink a lot of liquor?"

"Liquor?" said the man indignantly. "I never touch the filthy stuff."

"How about smoking?"

"I think smoking is disgusting. I've never in my life touched tobacco."

"I'm a bit embarrassed to ask this, but—you know the way some men are—do you do any running around at night?"

"Of course not. What do you take me for? I'm in bed every night by ten o'clock at the latest."

"Tell me," said the doctor, "the pain in the head you speak of, is it a sharp, shooting kind of pain?"

"Yes," said the man. "That's it—a sharp, shooting kind of pain."

"Simple, my dear fellow! Your trouble is you have your halo on too tight. All we need to do is loosen it a bit."[1]

The trouble with our ideals is that if we live up to all of them, we become impossible to live with.

The tilted halo of the saved sinner is worn loosely and with easy grace. We have discovered that the cross accomplished far more than revealing the love of God. The blood of the Lamb points to the truth of grace: what we cannot do for ourselves, God has done for us. On the cross, somehow, someway, Christ bore our sins, took our place, and died for us. At the cross, Jesus unmasks the sinner not only as a beggar but as a *criminal* before God. Jesus Christ bore our sins and bore them away. We cannot wash away the stain of our sins, but He is the Lamb who has taken away the sins of the world.

The sinner saved by grace is haunted by Calvary, by the cross, and especially by the question, *Why did He die?* A clue comes from the Gospel of John: "For this is how God loved the world: he gave his only Son, so that everyone who believes in him may not perish but may have eternal life." Another clue from Paul's cry in Galatians: "He loved me and delivered himself up for me." The answer lies in love.

But the answer seems too easy, too glib. Yes, God saved us because He loved us. But He is God. He has infinite imagination. Couldn't He have dreamed up a different redemption? Couldn't He have saved us with a smile, a pang of hunger, a word of forgiveness, a single drop of blood? And if He had to die, then for God's sake—for Christ's sake—couldn't He have died in bed, died with dignity? Why was He condemned like a criminal? Why was His back flayed with whips? Why was His head crowned with thorns? Why was He nailed to wood and allowed to die in frightful, lonely agony? Why was the last breath drawn in bloody disgrace, while the world for which He lay dying egged on His executioners with savage fury like some kind of gang rape by uncivilized brutes in Central Park? Why did they have to take the very best?

One thing we do know: We don't comprehend the love of Jesus Christ. Oh, we see a movie and resonate to what a young man and woman will endure for romantic love. We know that when the chips are down, if we love wildly enough we'll fling life and caution to the winds for the one we love. But when it comes to God's love in the broken, blood-drenched body of Jesus Christ, we get antsy and start to talk about theology, divine justice, God's wrath, and the heresy of universalism.

The saved sinner is prostrate in adoration, lost in wonder and praise. He knows repentance is not what we do in order to earn forgiveness; it is what we do because we have been for-given. It serves as an expression of gratitude rather than an effort to earn forgiveness. Thus the sequence of forgiveness and then repentance, rather than repentance and then forgiveness, is cru-cial for understanding the gospel of grace.

But many of us don't know our God and don't understand His gospel of grace. For many, God sits up there like a Buddha, impassive, unmoving, hard as flint. Calvary cries out more clearly than any theology textbook: *We do not know our*

God. We have not grasped the truth in the First Letter of John: "In this is love, not that we loved God but that He loved us and sent his Son to be the propitiation for our sins." The cross reveals the depth of the Father's love for us: "For greater love than this no one has than that he lay down his life for his friends."

The disciple living by grace rather than law has undergone a decisive conversion—*a turning from mistrust to trust.* The foremost characteristic of living by grace is trust in the redeeming work of Jesus Christ.

To believe deeply, as Jesus did, that God is present and at work in human life is to understand that I am a beloved child of this Father and, hence, *free to trust.* That makes a profound difference in the way I relate to myself and others; it makes an enormous difference in the way I live. To trust Abba, both in prayer and life, is to stand in childlike openness before a mystery of gracious love and acceptance.[2]

The tendency in legalistic religion is to mistrust God, to mistrust others, and consequently, to mistrust ourselves. Allow me to become personal for a moment. Do you really believe that the Father of our Lord and Savior Jesus Christ is gracious, that He cares about you? Do you really believe that He is always, unfailingly present to you as companion and support? Do you really believe that God is love?

Or have you learned to fear this loving and gracious Father? "In love," John says, "there is no room for fear, but perfect love drives out fear, because fear implies punishment and no one who is afraid has come to perfection in love" (1 John 4:18). Have you learned to think of the Father as the judge, the spy, the disciplinarian, the punisher? If you think that way, you are wrong.

The Father's love is revealed in the Son's. The Son has been given to us that we might give up fear. There is no fear in love. The Father sent the Son "that they may have life and have it to the full" (John 10:10). Is not the Son the Father's unsurpassable sign of love and graciousness? Did He not come to show us the Father's compassionate care for us? "Whoever sees me, sees the one who sent me" (John 12:45). The Father is not justice and the Son love. The Father is justice *and* love; the Son is love *and* justice.

Abba is not our enemy. If we think that, we are wrong.

Abba is not intent on trying and tempting and testing us. If we think that, we are wrong.

Abba does not prefer and promote suffering and pain. If we think that, we are wrong.

Jesus brings good news about the Father, not bad news.

We need a new kind of relationship with the Father that drives out fear and mistrust and anxiety and guilt, that permits us to be hopeful and joyous, trusting and compassionate. We have to be converted from the bad news to the good news, from expecting nothing to expecting something.[3] "The time is fulfilled," Jesus said, "and the kingdom of God is close at hand. Repent, and believe the gospel" (Mark 1:15). Turn away from the sins of skepticism and despair, mistrust and cynicism, complaining and worry.

The gospel of grace calls us to sing of the everyday mystery of intimacy with God instead of always seeking for miracles or visions. It calls us to sing of the spiritual roots of such commonplace experiences as falling in love, telling the truth, raising a child, teaching a class, forgiving each other after we have hurt each other, standing together in the bad weather of life, of surprise and sexuality, and the radiance of existence.[4] Of such is the kingdom of heaven, and of such homely mysteries is genuine religion made. The conversion from mistrust to trust is a confident quest seeking the spiritual meaning of human existence. Grace abounds and walks around the edges of our everyday experience.

Trust defines the meaning of living by grace rather than works. Trust is like climbing a fifty-foot ladder, reaching the top, and hearing someone down below yell, "Jump!" The trusting disciple has this childlike confidence in a loving Father. Trust says, in effect, "Abba, just on the basis of what You have shown me in Your Son, Jesus, I believe You love me. You have forgiven me. You will hold me and never let me go. Therefore, I trust You with my life."

Donald McCullough puts it this way:

Grace means that in the middle of our struggle the referee blows the whistle and announces the end of the game. We are declared winners and sent to the showers. It's over for all huffing, puffing piety to earn God's favor; it's finished for all sweat-soaked straining to secure self-worth; it's the end of all competitive scrambling to get ahead of others in the game. Grace means that God is on our side and thus we are victors regardless of how well we have played the game. We might as well head for the showers and the champagne celebration.[5]

The gospel declares that no matter how dutiful or prayerful we are, we can't save ourselves. What Jesus did was sufficient. To the extent that we are self-made saints like the Pharisees or neutral like Pilate (never making the leap in trust), we let the prostitutes and publicans go first into the kingdom while we, in Flannery O'Connor's unforgettable image, are in the background having our alleged virtue burnt out of us. The hookers and swindlers enter before us because they know they cannot save themselves, that they cannot make themselves presentable or lovable. They risked everything on Jesus and, knowing they didn't have it all together, were not too proud to accept the handout of amazing grace.

Maybe this is the heart of our hang-up, the root of our dilemma. We fluctuate between castigating ourselves and congratulating ourselves because we are deluded into thinking we save ourselves. We develop a false sense of security from our good works and scrupulous observance of the law. Our halo gets too tight and a carefully disguised attitude of moral superiority results. Or we are appalled by our inconsistency, devastated that we haven't lived up to our lofty expectations of ourselves. The roller coaster ride of elation and depression continues.

Why?

Because we never lay hold of our nothingness before God, and consequently, we never enter into the deepest reality of our relationship with Him. But when we accept ownership of our powerlessness and helplessness, when we acknowledge that we are paupers at the door of God's mercy, then God can make something beautiful out of us.

This poverty of spirit is the second major characteristic of saved sinners with tilted halos living by grace. What is the person canonized by Jesus in the first beatitude ("Blessed are those who know that they are poor") really like?

A story: Several years ago, at the end of a parish renewal in Algiers, Louisiana, a man of about forty approached me outside the church and muttered, "I've prayed about this." He slipped an envelope in my pocket and hurried away. I was overdue at a reception in the parish hall, so I jogged over to converse with folks, completely forgetting the envelope. Late that night in preparing for bed, I emptied my pockets, opened the envelope, and a check for six thousand dollars fell to the floor.

Prior to that renewal, I had lived for a few days at the city garbage dump in Juarez, Mexico, where little children and old men and women literally scavenged food from a mound of refuse more than thirty feet high. Several children died each week because of malnutrition and polluted water. I sent the six-thousand-dollar check to a man with ten children, three of whom had already died from the grinding poverty and wretched living conditions.

Do you know what the man who received the check did?

He wrote me nine letters in two days—letters overflowing with gratitude and describing in detail how he was using the money to help his own family and other neighbors at the dump. That gave me a beautiful insight into what a poor man is like.

When he receives a gift he first experiences, then expresses, genuine gratitude. Having nothing, he appreciates the slightest gift. I have been given the utterly undeserved gift of salvation in Jesus Christ. Through no merit of mine, I have been given a bona fide invitation to drink new wine forever at the wedding feast in the kingdom of God. (Incidentally, for a recovering alcoholic, that's heaven!)

But sometimes I get so involved with myself that I start making demands for things I think I deserve, or I take for granted every gift that comes my way. Classic case: Man in restaurant orders crabmeat salad; mistakenly, waitress brings shrimp salad; livid, angry man roars, "Where the hell's my crabmeat?" Somehow, life owes him a crabmeat salad. He takes for granted not only the shrimp salad but so many other gifts—life, faith, family, friends, talents.

The deeper we grow in the Spirit of Jesus Christ, the poorer we become—the more we realize that everything in life is a gift. The tenor of our lives becomes one of humble and joyful thanksgiving. Awareness of our poverty and ineptitude causes us to rejoice in the gift of being called out of darkness into wondrous light and translated into the kingdom of God's beloved Son. The poor man and woman write nine letters to the Lord that cry out, "It is right."

In conversation, the disciple who is truly poor in spirit always leaves the other person feeling, *My life has been enriched by talking with you.* This is neither false modesty nor phony humility. His or her life has been enriched and graced. He is not all exhaust and no intake. She does not impose herself on others. He listens well because he knows he has so much to learn from others. Her spiritual poverty enables her to enter the world of the other, even when she cannot identify with that world—e.g., the drug culture, the gay world. The poor in spirit are the most nonjudgmental of peoples; they get along well with sinners.

The poor man and woman of the gospel have made peace with their flawed existence. They are aware of their lack of wholeness, their brokenness, the simple fact that they don't have it all together. While they do not excuse their sin, they are humbly aware that sin is precisely what has caused them to throw themselves at the mercy of the Father. They do not pretend to be anything but what they are: sinners saved by grace.

The person who is poor in spirit realizes that he or she does not love others as much as his or her heart would wish. I once preached six weeklong Lenten renewals in succession. The last was in Downers Grove, Illinois, and on the closing night I was wiped out. Over one thousand people had attended. As the recessional song signaling my exit from the church began, I debated internally whether my body could handle another half-hour of farewells and blessings in the vestibule.

An attractive alternative loomed. I could flee to the sacristy, divest myself of the ministerial robes, grab a cold drink, run to my room, and crash. Spirit willing but flesh rebelling. Finally, I prayed for a zap of the Holy Spirit, opted for the farewells in the parish hall, got into it as best I could, and hit the boards around midnight.

The next morning, a note addressed to me lay on the breakfast table: "Dear Brennan, I attended your parish renewal all this week. You are eloquent, brilliant, poetic, witty, aesthetic, and…inflated. Last night when you stood in the parish hall after the service ended, where was the love in your eyes for each of us in the midst of your glory? Why didn't you stoop down and hug those little children? Why didn't you kiss the old ladies on the cheek? Why didn't you look at us from the core of your being, depth meeting depth, love meeting love? Man, are you blind!"

The letter was signed, "A mirror."

Obviously the person needed something that I didn't give. Under the circumstances, his or her expectations may have been unreasonable. But even when I am not tired, I realize that I don't love as much as I could or should or would. Often I will think of a thoughtful thing to say to a woman in a counseling session twenty minutes after she has walked out the door.

I will hear what a woman says and not what she means and wind up giving sage advice to a nonproblem. Distracted by a disturbing phone call, I left home to give a lecture to the inmates of Trenton State Penitentiary and began with the outrageous greeting, "Well, it's nice to see so many of you here."

And so it goes. Frequently not on top, in control, or as the Irish say, "in fine form." This is part of our poverty as human beings. When we have self-acceptance without self-concern we simply express reality. To be human is to be poor. Our impoverished spirit gives us pause before deciding to become tyrants to ourselves.[6]

Should you ask the biblically poor woman to describe her prayer life, she might answer, "Most of the time, my prayer consists in experiencing the absence of God in the hope of communion." She is not richly endowed with mystical experiences. That is fine because it reflects the truth of her impoverished humanity.

Yet the experience of absence does not mean the absence of experience. For example, the soldier in combat who, during a lull in the battle, steals a glance at his wife's picture tucked in his helmet, is more present to her at that moment in her absence than he is to the rifle that is present in his hands. Likewise, the poor in spirit perceive that religious experience and mystical "highs" are not the goal of authentic prayer; rather, the goal is communion with God.

The Christian who is truly poor in spirit goes to worship on Sunday morning singing, "I am poor but I brought myself the best I could. I am Yours, I am Yours."

Teresa of Avila, one of the great lights in the history of prayer, tells this story in her book *The Way of Perfection:*

> I know a nun who could not practice anything but vocal prayer… She came to me in great distress saying she did not know how to practice mental prayer, meditation, centering prayer and that she could not contemplate but only say vocal prayers. She was quite an old woman and had lived an extremely good and religious life. I asked her what prayers she said, and from her reply I saw that in simply saying the Lord's Prayer over and over, she was experiencing pure contemplation, and the Lord was raising her to be with him in union. So I praised the Lord and envied her vocal prayer.

The prayer of the poor in spirit can simply be a single word: *Abba.* Yet that word can signify dynamic interaction. Imagine a little boy trying to help his father with some household work, or making his mother a gift. The help may be nothing more than getting in the way, and the gift may be totally useless, but the love behind it is simple and pure, and the loving response it evokes is virtually uncontrollable. I am sure it is this way between our Abba and us. At the deepest, simplest levels, we just want each other to be happy, to be pleased. Our sincere desire counts far more than any specific success or failure. Thus when we try to pray and cannot, or when we fail in a sincere attempt to be compassionate, God touches us tenderly in return.

In this sense, there is no such thing as *bad* prayer.

A third characteristic of the tilted-halo gang is honesty. We must know who we are. How difficult it is to be honest, to accept that I am unacceptable, to renounce self-justification, to give up the pretense that my prayers, spiritual insight, tithing, and successes in ministry have made me pleasing to God! No antecedent beauty enamors me in His eyes. I am lovable only because He loves me.

Honesty is such a precious commodity that it is seldom found in the world or the church. Honesty requires the truthfulness to admit the attachment and addictions that control our attention, dominate our consciousness, and function as false gods. I can be addicted to vodka or to being nice, to tobacco or being loved, to cocaine or being right, to gambling or relationships, to golf or gossiping. Perhaps my addiction is food, performance, money, popularity, power, revenge, reading, television, weight, or winning. When we give anything more priority than we give to God, we commit idolatry. Thus we all commit idolatry countless times every day.

Once we accept the gospel of grace and seek to shed defense mechanisms and subterfuges, honesty becomes both more difficult and more important. Honesty involves the willingness to face the truth of who we are, regardless of how threatening or unpleasant our perceptions may be. It means hanging in there with ourselves and with God, learning our mind tricks by experiencing how they defeat us, recognizing our avoidances, acknowledging our lapses, learning completely that we cannot handle it ourselves. This steady self-confrontation requires strength and courage. We cannot use failure as an excuse to quit trying.[7]

Without personal honesty I can easily construct an image of myself that is rather impressive. Complacency will then replace delight in God. Many of us do not want the truth about ourselves; we prefer to be reassured of our virtue, as illustrated by this vignette.

One day a preacher said to a friend, "We have just had the greatest revival our church has experienced in many years."

"How many did you add to your church membership?"

"None. We lost five hundred."[8]

To be alive is to be broken. And to be broken is to stand in need of grace. Honesty keeps us in touch with our neediness and the truth that we are saved sinners. There is a beautiful transparency to honest disciples who never wear a false face and do not pretend to be anything but who they are.

When a man or woman is truly honest (not just working at it) it is virtually impossible to insult them personally. There is nothing there to insult. Those who were truly ready for the kingdom were just such people. Their inner poverty of spirit and rigorous honesty had set them free. They were people who had nothing to be proud of.

There was the sinful woman in the village who kissed Jesus' feet. There was freedom in doing that. Despised as a prostitute, she had accepted the truth of her utter nothingness before the Lord. She had nothing to lose. She loved much because much had been forgiven her.

The so-called Good Thief was a terrorist who acknowledged he was receiving the just reward of his crimes. He also had nothing to be proud of.

The Good Samaritan, chosen as the model of Christian compassion, was despised as a heretic of mixed pagan and Jewish ancestry. He was so unclean already that, unlike the priest and Levite who passed by with their halos on tight, he could afford to express his love for the wounded man left for dead.

Getting honest with ourselves does not make us unacceptable to God. It does not distance us from God, but draws us to Him—as nothing else can—and opens us anew to the flow of grace. While Jesus calls each of us to a more perfect life, we cannot achieve it on our own. To be alive is to be broken; to be broken is to stand in need of grace. It is only through grace that any of us could dare to hope that we could become more like Christ.

The saved sinner with the tilted halo has been converted from mistrust to trust, has arrived at an inner poverty of spirit, and lives as best he or she can in rigorous honesty with self, others, and God.

The question the gospel of grace puts to us is simply this: Who shall separate you from the love of Christ? What are you afraid of?

Are you afraid that your weakness could separate you from the love of Christ? It can't.

Are you afraid that your inadequacies could separate you from the love of Christ? They can't.

Are you afraid that your inner poverty could separate you from the love of Christ? It can't.

Difficult marriage, loneliness, anxiety over the children's future? They can't.

Negative self-image? It can't.

Economic hardship, racial hatred, street crime? They can't.

Rejection by loved ones or the suffering of loved ones? They can't.

Persecution by authorities, going to jail? They can't.

Nuclear war? It can't.

Mistakes, fears, uncertainties? They can't.

The gospel of grace calls out, *Nothing can ever separate you from the love of God made visible in Christ Jesus our Lord.*

You must be convinced of this, trust it, and never forget to remember. Everything else will pass away, but the love of Christ is the same yesterday, today, and forever. Faith will become vision, hope will become possession, but the love of Jesus Christ that is stronger than death endures forever.

In the end, it is the one thing you can hang onto.

Chapter Five

CORMORANTS AND KITTIWAKES

*S*everal years before his death, a remarkable rabbi, Abraham Joshua Heschel, suffered a near-fatal heart attack. His closest male friend was at his bedside. Heschel was so weak he was only able to whisper. "Sam," he said, "I feel only gratitude for my life, for every moment I have lived. I am ready to go. I have seen so many miracles during my lifetime." The old rabbi was exhausted by his effort to speak. After a long pause, he said, "Never once in my life did I ask God for success or wisdom or power or fame. I asked for wonder, and He gave it to me."

I asked for wonder, and He gave it to me. A Philistine will stand before a Claude Monet painting and pick his nose; a person filled with wonder will stand there fighting back the tears.

By and large, our world has lost its sense of wonder. We have grown up. We no longer catch our breath at the sight of a rainbow or the scent of a rose, as we once did. We have grown bigger and everything else smaller, less impressive. We get blasé and worldly-wise and sophisticated. We no longer run our fingers through water, no longer shout at the stars or make faces at the moon. Water is H_2O, the stars have been classified, and the moon is not made of green cheese. Thanks to satellite TV and jet planes, we can visit places once accessible only to a Columbus, a Balboa, and other daring explorers.

There was a time in the not too distant past when a thunderstorm caused grown men to shudder and feel small. But God is being edged out of His world by science. The more we know about meteorology, the less inclined we are to pray during a thunderstorm. Airplanes now fly above, below, and around them. Satellites reduce them to photographs. What ignominy—if a thunderstorm could experience ignominy! Reduced from theophany to nuisance!

Heschel says that today we believe all enigmas can be solved. As Samuel Johnson once said, wonder is nothing but "the effect of novelty upon ignorance." Certainly, the new can amaze us: a space shuttle, the latest computer game, the softest diaper. Till tomorrow, till the new becomes old, till yesterday's wonder is discarded or taken for granted. Small wonder Rabbi Heschel concluded, "As civilization advances, the sense of wonder declines."

We get so preoccupied with ourselves, the words we speak,

the plans and projects we conceive, that we become immune to the glory of creation. We barely notice the cloud passing over the moon or the dewdrops clinging to the rose petals. The ice on the pond comes and goes. The wild blackberries ripen and wither. The blackbird nests outside our bedroom window, but we don't see her. We avoid the cold and the heat. We refrigerate ourselves in summer and entomb ourselves in plastic in winter. We rake up every leaf as fast as it falls. We are so accustomed to buying prepackaged meats and fish and fowl in supermarkets, we never think and blink about the bounty of God's creation. We grow complacent and lead practical lives. We miss the experience of awe, reverence, and wonder.[1]

Our world is saturated with grace, and the lurking presence of God is revealed not only in spirit but in matter—in a deer leaping across a meadow, in the flight of an eagle, in fire and water, in a rainbow after a summer storm, in a gentle doe streaking through a forest, in Beethoven's Ninth Symphony, in a child licking a chocolate ice cream cone, in a woman with windblown hair. God intended for us to discover His loving presence in the world around us.

For several centuries the Celtic church of Ireland was spared the Greek dualism of matter and spirit. They regarded the world with the clear vision of faith. When a young Celtic monk saw his cat catch a salmon swimming in shallow water, he cried, "The power of the Lord is in the paw of the cat." The Celtic chronicles tell of the wandering sailor monks of the Atlantic, seeing the angels of God and hearing their song as they rose and fell over the western islands. To the scientific person they were only gulls and gannets, puffins, cormorants and kittiwakes. But the monks lived in a world in which everything was a word of God to them, in which the love of God was manifest to anyone with the least creative imagination. How else, they wondered, would God speak to them? They cherished the Scriptures, but they also cherished God's ongoing revelation in His world of grace. "Nature breaks through the eyes of a cat," they said.[2] For the eyes of faith, every created thing manifests the grace and providence of Abba.

So often we religious people walk amid the beauty and bounty of nature and we talk nonstop. We miss the panorama of color and sound and smell. We might as well have remained indoors in our closed, artificially lit living rooms. Nature's lessons are lost and the opportunity to be wrapped in silent wonder before the God of creation passes. We fail to be stretched by the magnificence of the world saturated with grace. Creation doesn't calm our troubled spirits, restore our perspective, or delight us in every part of our being.[3] It reminds us instead of mundane chores: changing the page on the calendar or ordering our snow tires. We must rediscover the gospel of grace and the world of grace.

For "the grace of our Lord Jesus Christ, the love of God and the fellowship of the Holy Spirit" opens us to the divine spread everywhere about us, especially in the life of a loving person.

I am thinking of the beggar in Molière's *Don Juan*. He sits at the corner of the street as a nobleman passes. The passing stranger is the aristocrat Don Juan, an embittered man, both his fortune and his character ruined.

"An alm for the love of God," cries the beggar.

Don Juan stops, reaches in his pocket and holds out his last gold coin above the outstretched arms of the beggar. "Blaspheme God," he says, "and I'll give it to you."

"O no, my Lord," says the beggar, "I would never do that."[4] A gesture like that is more grace-full than a heaven full of stars, a thousand symphonies, an Eiffel Tower, or a Mona Lisa. Thomas Aquinas said that the splendor of a soul in grace is so seductive that it surpasses the beauty of all created things.

A story is told about Fiorello LaGuardia, who, when he was mayor of New York City during the worst days of the Great Depression and all of World War II, was called "the Little Flower" by adoring New Yorkers because he was only five foot four and always wore a carnation in his lapel. He was a colorful character who used to ride the New York City fire trucks, raid speakeasies with the police department, take entire orphanages to baseball games, and whenever the New York newspapers were on strike, he would go on the radio and read the Sunday funnies to the kids.

One bitterly cold night in January of 1935, the mayor turned up at a night court that served the poorest ward of the city. LaGuardia dismissed the judge for the evening and took over the bench himself. Within a few minutes, a tattered old woman was brought before him, charged with stealing a loaf of bread. She told LaGuardia that her daughter's husband had deserted her, her daughter was sick, and her two grandchildren were starving. But the shopkeeper, from whom the bread was stolen, refused to drop the charges. "It's a bad neighborhood, Your Honor," the man told the mayor. "She's got to be punished to teach other people around here a lesson."

LaGuardia sighed. He turned to the woman and said, "I've

got to punish you. The law makes no exceptions—ten dollars or ten days in jail." But even as he pronounced the sentence, the mayor was already reaching into his pocket. He extracted a bill and tossed it into his famous sombrero, saying, "Here is the ten dollar fine, which I now remit; and furthermore I am going to fine everyone in this courtroom fifty cents for living in a town where a person has to steal bread so that her grandchildren can eat. Mr. Bailiff, collect the fines and give them to the defendant."

So the following day the New York City newspapers reported that $47.50 was turned over to a bewildered old lady who had stolen a loaf of bread to feed her starving grandchildren, fifty cents of that amount being contributed by the red-faced grocery store owner, while some seventy petty criminals, people with traffic violations, and New York City policemen, each of whom had just paid fifty cents for the privilege of doing so, gave the mayor a standing ovation.[5]

What an extraordinary moment of grace for everyone present in that courtroom! The grace of God operates at a profound level in the life of a loving person. Oh, that we would recognize God's grace when it comes to us!

Recently I directed a three-day silent retreat for six women in Virginia Beach. As the retreat opened, I met briefly with each woman and asked her to write on a sheet of paper the one grace that she would most like to receive from the Lord. A married woman from North Carolina, about forty-five years old, with an impressive track record of prayer and service to others, told me she wanted more than anything to actually experience just one time the love of God. I assured her that I would join her in that prayer.

The following morning this woman (whom I'll call Winky) arose before dawn and went for a walk on the beach, which was less than fifty yards from our house. Walking along the seashore barefoot, with the chilly waters of the Atlantic Ocean lapping against her feet and ankles, she noticed some one hundred yards away a teenage boy and a woman fifteen yards behind walking in her direction. In less than a minute the boy had passed by to her left, but the woman made an abrupt ninety-degree turn, walked straight toward Winky, embraced her deeply, and kissed her on the cheek. She whispered, "I love you," and continued on her way. Winky had never seen the woman before. Winky wandered along the beach for another hour before returning to the house. She knocked on my door. When I opened it, she was smiling. "Our prayer was answered," she said simply.

In his book *The Magnificent Defeat*, Frederick Buechner writes:

> For what we need to know, of course, is not just that God exists, not just that beyond the steely brightness of the stars there is a cosmic intelligence of some kind that keeps the whole show going, but that there is a God right here in the thick of our day-by-day lives who may not be writing messages about himself in the stars but in one way or another is trying to get messages through our blindness as we move around down here knee-deep in the fragrant muck and misery and marvel of the world. It is not objective proof of God's existence that we want but the experience of God's presence. That is

the miracle we are really after, and that is also, I think, the miracle that we really get.[6]

Living by the gospel of grace leads us into what Teilhard de Chardin called *the divine milieu*—a God-filled, Christ-soaked universe. A world charged with the grandeur of God. How do we live in the presence of the living God? In wonder, amazed by the traces of God all around us.

Grace abounds in contemporary movies, books, novels, films, and music. If God is not in the whirlwind, He may be in a Woody Allen film or a Bruce Springsteen concert. Most people understand imagery and symbol better than doctrine and dogma. Images touch hearts and awaken imaginations. One theologian suggested that Springsteen's *Tunnel of Love* album, in which he symbolically sings of sin, death, despair, and redemption, is more important for Catholics than the Pope's last visit when he spoke of morality only in doctrinal propositions. Troubadours have always been more important and influential than theologians and bishops.

Elsewhere in the media, in 1984 a modern version of the medieval morality play slipped into primetime television almost without anyone noticing it. In many ways Bill Cosby became the most influential religion teacher in America. Every week his program *The Cosby Show* presented vivid and appealing paradigms of love to vast audiences. This love was disclosed by the resolution of family tensions in the lives of characters who became as real to us as our next-door neighbors—Cliff, Claire, Sondra, Denise, Theo, Vanessa, Rudi, and so on. We learned, without even realizing it, how to live lovingly in families. We laughed at the familiar pattern of conflict and tension created by apparently trivial family crises like an engagement announcement, a fiftieth birthday, a big telephone bill, a fight between young lovers, a wedding anniversary of grandparents, a divorce between friends, an assault of the flu on the family. As we laughed, we saw the virtues required for conflict resolution like patience, trust, sensitivity, honesty, flexibility, and forgiveness.[7]

Family life has been the raw material of much of Cosby's humor from the beginning of his career, and it has always been a humor of love. Perhaps his doctorate in education made him more reflective about what he was doing, more conscious of the moral and spiritual issues he was tackling, but he has always been, in his own way, a vehicle of grace.

Grace makes a striking breakthrough in a novel called *The Moviegoer* by the Southern writer Walker Percy. He tells the story of a commuter on the way home from his successful job, a man who inexplicably feels bad in proportion to the many reasons he has to feel good. Suddenly he suffers a severe heart attack and is removed from the train at a station he has passed countless times before but never visited. When the commuter regains consciousness, he is in a strange hospital bed surrounded by unfamiliar people. As his eye wanders around the room, he catches sight of the hand spread out on the sheet in front of him. It is as if he had never seen his own hand until this moment—this extraordinary thing able to move this way and that, to open and close.

Percy goes on to speak about this awakening as a revelation, an experience of what theologians would call "natural grace." Through the heart attack the commuter was able to encounter himself and his life in a way he had not for years, absorbed as he was in what he calls "everydayness." The ordeal restored him to himself. The event is of enormous existential importance, for what he chooses to do with the experience will be the whole burden of his future. When he rode the train every day, he was gripped by a nameless despair. Now the catastrophe of the heart attack has liberated him from the paralysis of a living death and launched him on a search for meaning.[8]

In the hospital he keeps staring at his hand. The commuter says, "My hand was open in front of my face. The fingers closed and opened. I felt like Rip van Winkle waking up and testing his bones. Was anything broken? Was I still in one piece?"

Like Rip van Winkle waking up. Percy presents the catastrophe as a rough shaking out of sleep, a blast of cold air. It is only the reality of death that is powerful enough to quicken people out of the sluggishness of everyday life and into an active search for what life is really about. Percy plunges his heroes into disaster and ordeal, only to speak out of the whirlwind about the worst of times being the best of times, about the preferability of hurricanes over good weather, about the willing return of soldiers to their worst nightmares. Percy's people not only live through the catastrophe but discover in it the freedom to act and to be. The commuter grabs his own existence round the neck and begins to live a renewed life in an ordinary world that had not been cleansed of "everydayness."

Our gracious God speaks to us in this novel and issues a call "to choose between generativity and stagnation, between continuing to have an impact, or sitting around waiting to die." It is the language of grace, conversion, *metanoia,* put in contemporary terms since, as Percy says, the old words of grace have been devalued.

Was it this novel that inspired Erma Bombeck to write a column entitled "If I Had My Life to Live Over Again"? In it, she wrote:

> I would have invited friends over to dinner even if the carpet was stained and the sofa faded. I would have sat on the lawn with my children and not worried about grass stains. I would never have bought anything just because it was practical, wouldn't show soil or was guaranteed to last a lifetime. When my child kissed me impetuously, I would never have said, "Later. Now get washed up for dinner." There would have been more I love yous, more I'm sorrys, but mostly, given another shot at life, I would seize every minute, look at it and really see it, live it, and never give it back.

Once again, right in the middle of our daily newspaper, an echo of grace. Each moment of our existence, we are either growing into more or retreating into less. We are either living a little more or dying a little bit, as Norman Mailer put it.

The spirituality of wonder knows the world is charged with grace, that while sin and war, disease and death are terribly real, God's loving presence and power in our midst are even more real.

In the grasp of wonder, I am surprised, I'm enraptured. It's Moses before the burning bush "afraid to look at God" (Exodus 3:6). It's Stephen about to be stoned: "I can see…the Son of man standing at the right hand of God" (Acts 7:56). It's Michelangelo striking his sculptured Moses and commanding him, "Speak!" It's Ignatius of Loyola in ecstasy as he eyes the sky at night, Teresa of Avila ravished by a rose. It's doubting Thomas discovering his God in the wounds of Jesus, Mother Teresa spying the face of Christ in the tortured poor. It's America thrilling to footsteps on the moon, a child casting his kite to the wind. It's a mother looking with love at her new-born infant. It's the wonder of a first kiss.[9]

The gospel of grace is brutally devalued when Christians maintain that the transcendent God can only be properly honored and respected by denying the goodness and the truth and the beauty of the things of this world.

Amazement and rapture should be our reaction to the God revealed as Love.

For a moment allow me to sketch with broad strokes a biblical theology of divine agape. Israel's earliest concept of God was based on the covenant, the contract made on Mount Sinai. Through their spokesman, Moses, God said to the Israelites, "You will be my people, and I shall be your God." Yahweh is first perceived by the Jewish community as a personal, relating Being. Their concept of God was vastly superior to that of the pagans whose gods were quite human, fickle, capricious, erotic, as unpredictable as the forces with which they were identified—wind, storm, fertility, the nation, and so forth.

But Israel knew a holy God, transcending everything visible and tangible, yet personal. He was somehow reflected in things but was not to be identified with things. Exodus depicts God as stable, interested, a Rock of dependability among so many dependents.

Thus the Jews related to a covenant God who had initiated the contract, who had talked to Israel first, begotten her as a people, and given her a sense of identity. In this primitive stage of the relationship, Israel's God was calm, even cold. The qualities of interest, fidelity, and stability were appreciated, but warmth and radiance had not yet appeared. Yahweh was like the Rock of Gibraltar in the wind of changing events. He had a face but it was deadpan with a touch of benignity—reminiscent of Charlton Heston or James Arness as Marshal Matt Dillon—there was no sugar or fancy to Yahweh. He was firm, just, a basis for confidence: He was not easily diverted from walking a straight line down Main Street or pursuing a kidnapped child across the desert and through Indian country right into the heart of Mexico. Unrelenting dependability. Israel's election was utterly gratuitous. No need for Nell to wear makeup or fancy finery like the other seductive belles. Matt Dillon is not seduced. He chooses Nell freely, homely as she was, and that gave her a real sense of confidence. It was a little scary at times, even a bit unreal and inhuman.

Israel's concept of God needed clearer definition, for God is not inhuman but will wear humanity, as He ultimately does in Jesus, far beyond the limits of humanity as we know it, so that He can be everything we are and are not.

Now God raised up the prophets, burned into their consciousness a lively awareness of His presence, and sent them to reveal Him in a warmer, more passionate manner. Though Israel had played the prostitute whoring after false gods, the prophets cry the constancy of God in the face of human infidelity:

"Israel, don't ever be so foolish as to measure my love for you in terms of your love for me! Don't ever compare your thin, pallid, wavering, and moody love with my love, for I am God, not man."

Human love will always be a faint shadow of God's love. Not because it is too sugary or sentimental, but simply because it can never compare from whence it comes. Human love, with all its passion and emotion, is a thin echo of the passion/emotion love of Yahweh.

In the Sinai wilderness the covenant God was faithful and just. Israel was faithful. They were related. But if Israel became unfaithful, logic and human justice required no further pursuit of Yahweh. He sees the contract broken, picks up His briefcase, and walks out of court. The relationship is ended.

But we cannot apply human logic and justice to the living God. Human logic is based on human experience and human nature. Yahweh does not conform to this model. If Israel is unfaithful, God remains faithful against all logic and all limits of justice because He is.

Love clarifies the happy irrationality of God's conduct. Love tends to be irrational at times. It pursues despite infidelity. It blossoms into jealousy and anger—which betrays keen interest. The more complex and emotional the image of God becomes in the Bible, the bigger He grows, and the more we approach the mystery of His indefinability.

The *hesed* of Yahweh draws Israel into greater confidence. Justice says, "I owe you nothing, for you have broken the contract." But where justice ends, love begins and reveals that God is not interested merely in the dividends of the covenant. He is looking into the eyes of Israel from His depths to hers. He sees through the smokescreen of deeds good and bad to Israel herself. She glances up uneasily. "Who? Me?"

"Yes, you. I don't want the abstractions of relationship. I want your heart." (This is not the tone of contemporary spirituality. Many of us put God on Pier 40 as a niggling customs officer. He rifles through our moral suitcase to sort out our deeds, and then hands us a scorecard to tally up virtues and vices, so we can match baseball cards with Him on Judgment Day.)

According to Hosea, God is willing to maintain a relationship even when His spouse has become a coarse and vulgar prostitute. This same conviction is carried into the New Testament. The adulterous woman is brought before Jesus. The god of religious leaders, who never got over Hosea's contribution, is expected to judge her. She has been unfaithful and the divine posture embodied in leadership would stone her. The God of the Pharisees is interested in the contract, in justice first and foremost. *Let us kill the woman for the contract.* The person is expendable.

But in the man, Jesus, we see the human face of God, one in keeping with Old Testament revelation. He is interested in the woman. His love moves beyond justice and proves more salvific than spelling out the ground rules all over again.[10]

Unjust? To our way of thinking, yes. Thank God! I am wonderfully content with a God who doesn't deal with me as my sins deserve. On the last day when Jesus calls me by name, "Come, Brennan, blessed of my Father," it will not be because Abba is just, but because His name is mercy.

Will we ever understand the gospel of grace, the furious love of God, the world of grace in which we live? Jesus Christ is the scandal of God. When the Baptizer is imprisoned by Herod, he sends a couple of his followers to ask Jesus, "Are you the One who is to come into the world or should we wait for another?" Jesus says, "Go back and tell John what you have seen and heard: the blind see, the deaf hear, the lame walk, the poor have the gospel preached to them, the messianic era has erupted into history, and the love of my Father is revealed. Blessed is he who is not *scandalized* in me."

We should be astonished at the goodness of God, stunned that He should bother to call us by name, our mouths wide open at His love, bewildered that at this very moment we are standing on holy ground.

Every parable of mercy in the gospel was addressed by Jesus to His opponents: murmuring scribes, grumbling Pharisees, critical theologians, members of the Sanhedrin. They are the enemies of the gospel of grace, indignant because Jesus asserts that God cares about sinners, incensed that He should eat with people they despised. What does He tell them?

These sinners, these people you despise are nearer to God than you. It is not the hookers and thieves who find it most difficult to repent. It is you who are so secure in your piety and pretense that you have no need of conversion. They may have disobeyed God's call, their professions have debased them, but they have shown sorrow and repentance. But more than any of that, these are the people who appreciate His goodness: They are parading into the kingdom before you for they have what you lack—a deep gratitude for God's love and deep wonder at

His mercy.

Let us ask God for the gift He gave to an unforgettable rabbi, Joshua Abraham Heschel: "Dear Lord, grant me the grace of wonder. Surprise me, amaze me, awe me in every crevice of Your universe. Delight me to see how Your Christ plays in ten thousand places, lovely in limbs, and lovely in eyes not His, to the Father through the features of men's faces. Each day enrapture me with Your marvelous things without number. I do not ask to see the reason for it all; I ask only to share the wonder of it all."

Chapter Six

GRAZIE, SIGNORE

*J*n his book *Mortal Lessons,* Richard Selzer, MD, writes:

I stand by the bed where a young woman lies, her face postoperative, her mouth twisted in palsy, clownish. A tiny twig of the facial nerve, the one to the muscles of her mouth, has been severed. She will be thus from now on. The surgeon had followed with religious fervor the curve of her flesh; I promise you that. Nevertheless, to remove the tumor in her cheek, I had to cut the little nerve.

Her young husband is in the room. He stands on the opposite side of the bed and together they seem to dwell in the evening lamplight, isolated from me, private. Who are they, I ask myself, he and this wry mouth I have made, who gaze at and touch each other so generously, greedily? The young woman speaks.

"Will my mouth always be like this?" she asks.

"Yes," I say, "it will. It is because the nerve was cut." She nods and is silent. But the young man smiles.

"I like it," he says, "It is kind of cute."

All at once I *know* who he is. I understand and I lower my gaze. One is not bold in an encounter with a god. Unmindful, he bends to kiss her crooked mouth and I am so close I can see how he twists his own lips to accommodate to hers, to show her that their kiss still works.[1]

Since reading this passage, the image of the husband contorting his mouth and twisting his lips for an intimate kiss with his palsied wife haunted me. Yet something eluded me until, one day in prayer, it exploded anew in my memory of the violence on a hill outside the city wall of old Jerusalem. The mangled body of the Son hangs exposed to the world's derision. He is a blasphemer of God and a seducer of the people. Let Him die in disgrace. His friends are scattered, His honor broken, His name a laughingstock. He has been forsaken by His God. Left absolutely alone. Drive Him out of the holy city and across the tracks where His kind belong. The ragamuffin Christ is roughly handled, pushed around, scourged and spat upon, murdered and buried among His own ilk.

In order to dramatize His death, some Christian artists have given the crucified Christ a rolling eye and a contorted mouth; they use red lead to make realistic drops of blood flow from His hands, feet, and side.

In 1963 a friend gave me an expensive crucifix. A French artist had carved in wood, carved very delicately, the hands of Jesus on the cross. On Good Friday the Roman artists carved— O God, how they carved!—our brother Jesus with no trouble at all. No art was needed to bang in the nails with hammers, no red lead to make real blood gush from His hands, feet, and side. His mouth was contorted and His lips twisted simply by hoisting Him up on the crossbeam. We have so theologized the passion and death of this sacred man that we no longer see the slow unraveling of His tissue, the spread of gangrene, His raging thirst.

In his monumental work *The Crucified God*, Jürgen Moltmann writes, "We have made the bitterness of the cross, the revelation of God in the cross of Jesus Christ, tolerable to ourselves by learning to understand it as a necessity for the process of salvation."[2]

I stroll down Royal Street in the French Quarter in New Orleans. Adjacent to the infamous Bourbon Street with its jazz emporiums, T-shirt stores, and sex boutiques, Royal is studded with antique shops. "Come look at this," says the antique dealer. "The Venus costs more, but this ivory Christ crucified is beautiful in its own way, especially against a black velvet backdrop." And the more we reproduce Him, the more we forget about Him and the agony of His third hour. We turn Him into gold, silver, ivory, marble, or whatever to free ourselves from His agony and death as a man.

"For our sake he made the sinless one a victim for sin, so that in him we might become the uprightness of God" (2 Corinthians 5:21). Every form of sin and its consequences, sickness and disease of every kind, drug addiction, alcoholism, broken relationships, insecurity, hatred, lust, pride, envy, jealousy, cancer, bone disease, arthritis, and on and on were experienced and carried by "one from whom, as it were, we averted our gaze, despised, for whom we had no regard" (Isaiah 53:3) who knew the nadir of an agony such as no one has ever dreamed. "I mean, God was in Christ reconciling the world to himself, not holding anyone's faults against them, but entrusting to us the message of reconciliation" (2 Corinthians 5:19). Jesus Christ nailed to the wood has carried our pain into the peace of grace. He has made peace through the blood of His cross (see Colossians 1:20).

Jesus has journeyed to the far reaches of loneliness. In His broken body He has carried your sins and mine, every separation and loss, every heart broken, every wound of the spirit that refuses to close, all the riven experiences of men, women, and children across the bands of time.

Jesus is God. You and I were fashioned from the clay of the earth and the kiss of His mouth.

What shall we say to such an outpouring of love? How shall we respond?

First, the love of Christ and His gospel of grace calls for a personal, free, and unconventional decision. To respond is to acknowledge that the other has taken the initiative and issued the invitation. The other's overture has made a response necessary.

However, the other is not some itinerant salesperson at the door peddling bric-a-brac. It is Christ offering the opportunity of a lifetime: "I have come into the world as light, to prevent anyone who believes in me from staying in the dark any more" (John 12:46).

There is an extraordinary power in storytelling that stirs the imagination and makes an indelible impression on the mind. Jesus employs a set of stories, known as the "crisis" parables to issue a warning, a summons to repentance, because of the lateness of the hour. Jesus says, "A tidal wave is approaching and you are lollygagging on the patio having a party." Or as Joachim Jeremias puts it, "You are feasting and dancing—on the volcano which may erupt at any moment."[3] The impending crisis precludes procrastination: "Stay awake, because you do not know when the master of the house is coming, evening, midnight, cockcrow, dawn; if he comes unexpectedly, he must not find you asleep. And what I say to you, I say to all: 'Stay awake!'"

In the parable of the wedding feast, the guest without a wedding garment is forcibly seized by the bouncers and heaved out the door. "The festal garment is repentance. Put it on today before your death, the day before the Deluge breaks, put it on today! The demand of the crisis is conversion."[4]

Rome is burning, Jesus says. *Drop your fiddle, change your life, and come to Me.* When a tornado comes tearing down the street, it is not time to stop and smell the flowers. Let go of the good old days that never were—a regimented church you never attended, traditional virtues you never practiced, legalistic obedience you never honored, and a sterile orthodoxy you never accepted. The old era is done. The decisive inbreak of God has happened.

The person who realizes the gravity of the situation knows that the decision brooks no delay. The Storyteller calls us not to fear but to action. Don't cling to cheap, painted fragments of glass when the pearl of great price is being offered. When a person's very existence is threatened, when he or she stands on the threshold of moral ruin, when everything is at stake, the hour has struck for bold and resolute decision-making.

In the parable of the talents, the three servants are called to render an account of how they have used the gifts entrusted to them. The first two used their talents boldly and resourcefully. The third, who prudently wraps his money and buries it, typifies the Christian who deposits his faith in an hermetic container and seals the lid shut. He or she limps through life on childhood memories of Sunday school and resolutely refuses the challenge of growth and spiritual maturity. Unwilling to take risks, this person loses the talent entrusted to him or her. "The master wanted his servants to take risks. He wanted them to gamble with his money."[5]

In a parable that was patently provocative to His Jewish audience, Jesus told the story of the crafty steward. We are presented with an embezzler who, to cover his tracks, launders his employer's money by falsifying his accounts. And Jesus praises the criminal!

> "There was a rich man and he had a steward who was denounced to him for being wasteful with his property. He called for the man and said, 'What is this I hear about you? Draw me an account of your stewardship because you are not to be my steward any longer.' Then the steward said to himself, 'Now that my master is taking the stewardship from me, what am I to do? Dig? I

am not strong enough. Go begging? I should be too ashamed. Ah, I know what I will do to make sure that when I am dismissed from office there will be some to welcome me into their homes.'

"Then he called his master's debtors one by one. To the first he said, 'How much do you owe my master?' 'One hundred measures of oil,' he said. The steward said, 'Here, take your bond; sit down and quickly write fifty.' To another he said, 'And you, sir, how much do you owe?' 'One hundred measures of wheat,' he said. The steward said, 'Here, take your bond and write eighty.'

"The master praised the dishonest steward for his astuteness. 'For the children of this world are more astute in dealing with their own kind than are the children of light.'" (Luke 16:1–8)

Men and women whose outlook on life is conditioned by the Dow are shrewder on the street than are the disciples on their spiritual journey. Unbelievers put us to shame. Imitate their shrewdness!

Jesus did not excuse the steward's action but admired his initiative. He did not let a tragic sequence of events unfold but did what he had to do, however unscrupulously, to make a new life for himself. Without illusions, he makes the most of the little time that remains.

The unjust steward who, hearing he is going to be fired, doctors his master's accounts to secure another job, is commended precisely because he acted. The point does not concern morality but apathy. Here is a man who finds himself in a crisis and, instead of wallowing in self-pity, acts resourcefully. The guests who do not respond to the King's banquet are quickly rejected and others are summoned. *Immediate response is the mood of the kingdom.* Imaginative shock issues an invitation which leads to decision and action.[6]

Most of us postpone a decision hoping that Jesus will get weary of waiting and the inner voice of Truth will get laryngitis. Thus, the summons of the crisis parables remains suspended in a state of anxiety, so long as we opt neither for nor against the new dimension of living open to us. Our indecision creates more problems than it solves. Indecision means we stop growing for an indeterminate length of time; we get stuck. With the paralysis of analysis, the human spirit begins to shrivel. The conscious awareness of our resistance to grace and the refusal to allow God's love to make us who we really are brings a sense of oppression. Our lives become fragmented, inconsistent, lacking in harmony and out of sync. The worm turns. The felt security of staying in a familiar place vanishes. We are caught between a rock and hard place. How do we resolve this conundrum?

We don't.

We cannot will ourselves to accept grace. There are no magic words, preset formulas, or esoteric rites of passage. Only Jesus Christ sets us free from indecision. The Scriptures offer no other basis for conversion than the personal magnetism of the Master.

One morning, mysteriously moved by grace, a young man decides to try prayer. For five minutes he agrees to show up and shut up. And Jesus whispers, *Now is the time! The unreal world of glasnost and Gucci loafers, Häagen-Dazs ice cream and Calvin Klein jeans, beaver vests, Persian rugs, silk underwear, and the Super Bowl is passing away. Now is the time to stop running around frantically like Lancelot's horse in four directions at once and quietly remember that only one thing is necessary. Now is the time for personal decision and creative response to My word.*

Let Me tell you a little story. One year a rich fool had a bonanza crop and made provisions for an even bigger one the following year. He said to himself, "You're a good ol' boy. You've worked hard, deserve everything that's coming to you, and have a nest egg for the future. Take it easy, eat heartily, drink up a storm, and have a good time."

That night my Father shattered his security: "Fool! This very night the demand will be made for your soul; and this hoard of yours, who is going to enjoy it now?"

In prayer Jesus slows us down, teaches us to count how few days we have, and gifts us with wisdom. He reveals to us that we are so caught up in what is urgent that we have overlooked what is essential. He ends our indecision and liberates us from the oppression of false deadlines and myopic vision.

Second, our response to the love of Jesus demands trust. Do we rely on our résumé or the gospel of grace? How do we cope with failure?

> Grace tells us that we are accepted just as we are. We may not be the kind of people we want to be, we may be a long way from our goals, we may have more failures

than achievements, we may not be wealthy or powerful or spiritual, we may not even be happy, but we are nonetheless accepted by God, held in his hands. Such is his promise to us in Jesus Christ, a promise we can trust.[7]

For those who feel their lives are a grave disappointment to God, it requires enormous trust and reckless, raging confidence to accept that the love of Christ knows no shadow of alteration or change. When Jesus said, "Come to me, all you who labor and are heavy burdened," He assumed we would grow weary, discouraged, and disheartened along the way. These words are a touching testimony to the genuine humanness of Jesus. He had no romantic notion of the cost of discipleship. He knew that following Him was as unsentimental as duty, as demanding as love. He knew that physical pain, the loss of loved ones, failure, loneliness, rejection, abandonment, and betrayal would sap our spirits; that the day would come when faith would no longer offer any drive, reassurance, or comfort; that prayer would lack any sense of reality or progress; that we would echo the cry of Teresa of Avila: "Lord, if this is the way you treat your friends, no wonder you have so few!"

For the high priest we have is not incapable of feeling our weaknesses with us, but has been put to the test in exactly the same way as ourselves, apart from sin. Let us, then, have no fear in approaching the throne of grace to receive mercy and to find grace when we are in need of help. (Hebrews 4:15–16)

A poet has written, "The desire to feel loved is the last illusion: let it go and you will be free." Just as the sunrise of faith requires the sunset of our former unbelief, so the dawn of trust requires letting go of our craving spiritual consolations and tangible reassurances. Trust at the mercy of the response it receives is a bogus trust. All is uncertainty and anxiety. In trembling insecurity the disciple pleads for proofs from the Lord that her affection is returned. If she does not receive them, she is frustrated and starts to suspect that her relationship with Jesus is all over or that it never even existed.

If she does receive consolation, she is reassured, but only for a time. She presses for further proofs—each one less convincing than the one that went before. In the end the need to trust dies of pure frustration. What the disciple has not learned is that tangible reassurances, however valuable they may be, cannot create trust, sustain it, or guarantee any certainty of its presence. Jesus calls us to hand over our autonomous self in unshaken confidence. When the craving for reassurances is stifled, trust happens.

The mystery of Jesus' ascension into heaven contains an important lesson. He said to His disciples: "I am telling you the truth: it is for your own good that I am going" (John 16:7). Why? How could Jesus' departure profit the apostles? Because while He was still visible on earth, there was the danger they would be too wedded to the sight of His flesh, that they would leave the certainty of faith and lean upon the tangible evidence of the senses. To see Jesus in the flesh was good but "blessed are those who have not seen and yet believe" (John 20:29).

When we wallow in guilt, remorse, and shame over real or

imagined sins of the past, we are disdaining God's gift of grace.

Preoccupation with self is always a major component of unhealthy guilt and recrimination. It stirs our emotions, churning in self-destructive ways, closes us in upon the mighty citadel of self, leads to depression and despair, and preempts the presence of a compassionate God. The language of unhealthy guilt is harsh. It is demanding, abusing, criticizing, rejecting, accusing, blaming, condemning, reproaching, and scolding. It is one of impatience and chastisement. Christians are shocked and horrified because they have failed. Unhealthy guilt becomes bigger than life. The image of the childhood story of Chicken Little comes to mind. Guilt becomes the experience in which people feel the sky is falling.

Yes, we feel guilt over sins, but healthy guilt is one which acknowledges the wrong done and feels remorse, but then is free to embrace the forgiveness that has been offered. Healthy guilt focuses on the realization that all has been forgiven, the wrong has been redeemed.

> We all have shadows and skeletons in our backgrounds. But listen, there is something bigger in this world than we are and that something bigger is full of grace and mercy, patience and ingenuity. The moment the focus of your life shifts from your badness to his goodness and the question becomes not "What have I done?" but "What can he do?" release from remorse can happen; miracle of miracles, you can forgive yourself because you are forgiven, accept yourself because you are accepted, and begin to start building up the

very places you once tore down. There is grace to help in every time of trouble. That grace is the secret to being able to forgive ourselves. Trust it.[8]

Perhaps you've heard this story: Several years ago in a large city in the far West, rumors spread that a certain Catholic woman was having visions of Jesus. The reports reached the archbishop. He decided to check her out. There is always a fine line between the authentic mystic and the lunatic fringe.

"Is it true, ma'am, that you have visions of Jesus?" asked the cleric.

"Yes," the woman replied simply.

"Well, the next time you have a vision, I want you to ask Jesus to tell you the sins that I confessed in my last confession."

The woman was stunned. "Did I hear you right, bishop? You actually want me to ask Jesus to tell me the sins of your past?"

"Exactly. Please call me if anything happens."

Ten days later the woman notified her spiritual leader of a recent apparition. "Please come," she said.

Within the hour the archbishop arrived. He trusted eye-to-eye contact. "You just told me on the telephone that you actually had a vision of Jesus. Did you do what I asked?"

"Yes, bishop, I asked Jesus to tell me the sins you confessed in your last confession."

The bishop leaned forward with anticipation. His eyes narrowed.

"What did Jesus say?"

She took his hand and gazed deep into his eyes. "Bishop,"

she said, "these are His exact words: 'I CAN'T REMEMBER.'"

Christianity happens when men and women accept with unwavering trust that their sins have not only been forgiven but forgotten, washed away in the blood of the Lamb. Thus, my friend archbishop Joe Reia says, "A sad Christian is a phony Christian, and a guilty Christian is no Christian at all."

The conversion from mistrust to trust is wrought at the foot of the cross. "Upon the Calvary of Christ's death the saints meditate, contemplate, and experience their Lord."[9] There is an essential connection between experiencing God, loving God, and trusting God. You will trust God only as much as you love Him. And you will love Him to the extent you have touched Him, rather that He has touched you.

Several years ago an anxious, fearful man in his midthirties came to a retreat I preached. A group of men who had known him for several years were on the same retreat and were astounded by the way they saw him change. Even his facial expression was transformed. Suddenly he had become free to trust. The basic experience was the deep realization that God loved him. It occurred through prayer. He was deeply moved by the words of Paul: "So it is proof of God's own love for us, that Christ died for us while we were still sinners" (Romans 5:8). His experience of human love had not the power to free him from mistrust as did that simple prayer before the crucified Christ.

The cross is a confrontation with the overwhelming good-ness of God revealed in the broken body of His only begotten Son. Our personal encounter, not simply the intellectual cogni-tion, but the experiential awareness of the love of Jesus Christ, propels us to trust. More than three hundred years ago, Claude de la Columbiere, commenting on the dinner Jesus attended in the home of Simon the Pharisee, wrote, "It is certain that of all those present, the one who most honors the Lord is Magdalene, who is so persuaded of the infinite mercy of God that all her sins appear to her as but an atom in the presence of this mercy."

The prophetic word spoken by Jesus to a thirty-four-year-old widow, Marjory Kempe, in Lynn, Massachusetts, in 1667 remains ever ancient, ever new: "More pleasing to Me than all your prayers, works, and penances is that you would believe I love you."

The grace to let go and let God be God flows from trust in His boundless love. "Since he did not spare his own Son, but gave him up for the sake of all of us, then can we not expect that with him he will freely give us all his gifts?" (Romans 8:32). Yet many of us find it exceedingly difficult to trust. Perhaps haunted by the specter of parents who lived in poverty, indoctrinated by slogans like "In God we trust; everybody else pays cash" and songs such as "Jesus Saves His Money at the Chase Manhattan Bank," we grew up with a skeptical spirit and assumed managerial control of our destiny.

Only love empowers the leap in trust, the courage to risk everything on Jesus, the readiness to move into the darkness guided only by a pillar of fire. Trust clings to the belief that whatever happens in our lives is designed to teach us holiness. The love of Christ inspires trust to thank God for the nagging headache, the arthritis that is so painful, the spiritual darkness that envelops us; to say with Job, "If we take happiness from God's hand, must we not take sorrow too?" (Job 2:10); to pray, with Charles Foucauld:

Abba, I abandon myself into your hands. Do with me
what you will. Whatever you may do, I thank you. I am
ready for all: I accept all. Let your will be done in me
and in all your creatures. I wish no more than this, O
Lord. Into your hands I commend my spirit. I offer it to
you with all the love of my heart, for I love you, Lord,
and I give myself, surrender myself into your hands
without reserve, with boundless confidence, *for you are
my Father.*

A Bahamian priest related a story that captures the essence of
biblical trust:

A two-story house had caught on fire. The family—
father, mother, several children—were on their way out
when the smallest boy became terrified, tore away from
his mother, ran back upstairs. Suddenly he appeared at a
smoke-filled window, crying like crazy. His father, outside, shouted, "Jump, son, jump! I'll catch you." The boy
cried, "But, daddy, I can't see you." "I know," his father
called, "I know. But I can see you."[10]

The third characteristic of our response to the gratuitous
intervention of Jesus in our lives is heartfelt gratitude.

In O. Henry's famous short story "The Gift of the Magi,"
the young wife has only $1.87 to buy her husband a gift, and
Christmas is the next day. Impulsively she decides to sell her
long, thick hair to buy him a chain for this treasured gold
watch. At the same moment he is selling the watch to buy his

present for her—special combs for her beautiful hair.

Have you ever done such an extravagant thing spontaneously? Gone off and emptied the piggy bank because a certain gift was perfect for someone you cherished?

> He was at Bethany in the house of Simon, a man who had suffered from a virulent skin-disease; he was at table when a woman came in with an alabaster jar of very costly ointment, pure nard. She broke the jar and poured the ointment on his head. Some who were there said to one another indignantly, "Why this waste of ointment? Ointment like this could have been sold for over three hundred denarii and the money given to the poor"; and they were angry with her. But Jesus said, "Leave her alone. Why are you upsetting her? What she has done for me is a good work. You have the poor with you always, and you can be kind to them whenever you wish, but you will not always have me. She has done what she could: she has anointed my body beforehand for its burial. In truth I tell you, wherever throughout all the world the gospel is proclaimed, what she has done will be told as well, in remembrance of her." (Mark 14:3–9)

What an impulsive, lovely gesture of gratitude! By human reckoning it was a foolish and wasteful thing to do. Yet Jesus was so deeply moved He wanted the tale of this woman's recklessness told and retold across the generations until the end of time.

Obviously, Jesus is saying there is a real place for the

impulsive and spontaneous, the lavish and impractical, the heroic and extraordinary, the unrestrained and incalculable bursts of generosity that cry out, "It is right to give You thanks and praise." Yet our gratitude to Jesus is, for the most part, our unsung service to those around us. "In truth I tell you, in so far as you did this to one of the least of these brothers of mine, you did it to me" (Matthew 25:40).

Though Christ no longer visibly moves among us, we minister to Him in the ragamuffins within reach. Each encounter with a brother or sister is a mysterious encounter with Jesus Himself. In the upper room, the Man like us in all things but ungratefulness spelled out the game plan of gratitude: "Love one another as I have loved you." To Peter on the beach along the Sea of Tiberias, He said, "If you love me, Simon, Son of John, tend my sheep." Quite simply, our deep gratitude to Jesus Christ is manifested neither in being chaste, honest, sober, and respectable, nor in churchgoing, Bible-toting, and Psalm-singing, but in our deep and delicate respect for one another.

Even Sunday worship is subordinated to reconciliation with others. "If you are bringing your offering to the altar and there remember that your brother has something against you, leave your offering there before the altar, go and be reconciled with your brother first, and then come back and present your offering" (Matthew 5:23–24).

Worship, cult, and religion in general have no absolute autonomy of their own for Jesus. God is a Being for others, not a Being for Himself alone. "Cultic worship is not only hypocritical but absolutely meaningless if it is not accompanied by love for other people; for in such a way it cannot possibly be a way of giving thanks to God."[11]

The ministry of evangelization is an extraordinary opportunity of showing gratitude to Jesus by passing on His gospel of grace to others. However, the "conversion by concussion" method, with one sledgehammer blow of the Bible after another, betrays a basic disrespect for the dignity of the other and is utterly alien to the gospel imperative to bear witness. To evangelize a person is to say to him or her, *You, too, are loved by God in the Lord Jesus.* And not only to say it but to really think it and relate it to the man or woman so they can sense it. This is what it means to announce the Good News. *But that becomes possible only by offering the person your friendship*—a friendship that is real, unselfish, without condescension, full of confidence, and profound esteem.

Amadeus was a remarkable film centered on two powerful and contrasting figures: Antonio Salieri, court composer to the Austrian emperor, and Wolfgang Amadeus Mozart, a brash and conceited young genius. "Someone described his life as wine, women and song. And he didn't sing much."[12] The limited, uninspired Salieri lives with a raging jealousy for the limitless, God-given talent of Mozart. Yet after every laborious score that he writes, Salieri whispers, "Grazie, Signore." *Thank You, Lord.* This song of Salieri lies at the heart of our response to the graciousness of God and the gospel of grace.

Grazie, Signore, for Your lips twisted in love to accommodate my sinful self; for judging me not by my shabby good deeds but by Your love that is Your gift to me; for Your unbearable forgiveness and infinite patience with me; for other people who have greater gifts than mine; and for the honesty to acknowledge that I am a ragamuffin. When the final curtain falls and You summon me home, may my last whispered word on earth be the wholehearted cry, "Grazie, Signore."

Chapter Seven

PASTE JEWELRY AND
SAWDUST HOT DOGS

*C*ounterfeit grace is as commonplace as fake furs, phony antiques, paste jewelry, and sawdust hot dogs. The temptation of the age is to look good without being good. If "white lies" were criminal offenses, we would all be in jail by nightfall. It took a lot of cooperation to create the atmosphere wherein the Charlotte and Baton Rouge televangelist scandals finally blossomed. The dichotomy between what we say and what we do is so pervasive in the church and in society that we actually come to believe our illusions and rationalizations and clutch them to our hearts like favorite teddy bears.

The HUD disgrace that rocked the nation's capital in 1989 caused Meg Greenfield to write in *Newsweek:*

The particularly cynical feature of this case is that people who have made a career, and a pretty successful career at that, of inveighing against corruption, mismanagement and near criminal incompetence that in fact do afflict some big government enterprises, have joined the opposition. The HUD scandal was particularly gross because it was an inside job and because it was so eminently a betrayal of the very values to which their administration claimed a unique loyalty.

Impostors in the Spirit always prefer appearances to reality. Rationalization begins with a look in the mirror. We don't like the sight of ourselves as we really are, so we try cosmetics, makeup, the right light, and the proper accessories to develop an acceptable image of ourselves. We rely on the stylish disguise that has made us look good or at least look away from our true self. Self-deception mortgages our sinfulness and prevents us from seeing ourselves as we really are—ragamuffins.

One of my indelible memories goes back to April 1975 when I was a patient at an alcoholic rehabilitation center in a small town north of Minneapolis. The setting was a large, split-level recreation room on the brow of a hill overlooking an artificial lake. Twenty-five chemically dependent men were assembled. Our leader was a trained counselor, skilled therapist, and senior member of the staff. His name was Sean Murphy-O'Connor, though he normally announced his arrival with the statement, "It's himself. Let's get to work."

Sean directed a patient named Max to sit on "the hot seat" in the center of the U-shaped group. A small, diminutive

man, Max was a nominal Christian, married with five children, owner and president of his company, wealthy, affable,
and gifted with remarkable poise.

"How long have you been drinking like a pig, Max?"
Murphy-O'Connor had begun the interrogation.

Max winced. "That's quite unfair."

"We shall see. I want to get into your drinking history. How
much booze per day?"

Max relit his corncob pipe. "I have two Marys with the
men before lunch and twin Martins after the office closes at
five. Then…"

"What are Marys and Martins?" Murphy-O'Connor inter-
rupts.

"Bloody Marys—vodka, tomato juice, a dash of lemon and
Worcestershire, a splash of Tabasco; and Martinis—Beefeater
gin, extra dry, straight up, ice-cold with an olive and lemon
twist."

"Thank you, Mary Martin. Continue."

"The wife likes a drink before dinner. I got her hooked on
Martins several years ago. Of course, she calls them 'preprandi-
als.'" Max smiled. "Of course, you understand the euphemism.
Isn't that right, gentlemen?"

No one responded.

"As I was saying, we have two martinis before dinner and
two more before going to bed."

"A total of eight drinks a day, Max?" Murphy-O'Connor
inquired.

"Absolutely right. Not a drop more, not a drop less."

"You're a liar!"

Unruffled, Max replied, "I'll pretend I didn't hear that. I have been in business for twenty-odd years and built my reputation on veracity, not mendacity. People know my word is my bond."

"Ever hide a bottle in your house?" asked Benjamin, a Navajo from New Mexico.

"Don't be ridiculous. I've got a bar in my living room as big as a horse." Max felt he had regained control. He was smiling again.

"Do you keep any booze in the garage, Max?"

"Naturally. I have to replenish the stock. A man in my profession does a lot of entertaining at home." The executive swagger had returned.

"How many bottles in the garage?"

"I really don't know the actual count. Offhand, I would say two cases of Smirnoff vodka, a case of Beefeater gin, a few bottles of bourbon and scotch, and a bevy of liquors."

The interrogation continued for another twenty minutes. Max fudged and hedged, minimized, rationalized, and justified his drinking pattern. Finally, hemmed in by relentless cross-examination, he admitted he kept a bottle of vodka in the nightstand, a bottle of gin in the suitcase for travel purpose, another in his bathroom cabinet for medicinal purposes, and three more at the office for entertaining clients. He squirmed occasionally but never lost his veneer of confidence.

Max grinned. "Gentlemen, I guess we have all gilded the lily once or twice in our lives" was the way he put it, implying that only men of large mien can afford the luxury of self-deprecating humor.

"You're a liar!" another voice boomed.

"No need to get vindictive, Charlie," Max shot back. "Remember the image in John's Gospel about the speck in your brother's eye and the two-by-four in your own. And the other one in Matthew about the pot calling the kettle black."

(I felt constrained to inform Max that the speck-and-plank comparison was not found in John but in Matthew and the pot and the kettle was a secular proverb found in none of the Gospels. But I sensed a spirit of smugness and an air of spiritual superiority had suddenly enveloped me like a thick fog. I decided to forgo the opportunity for fraternal correction. After all, I was not at Hazelden doing research on a book. I was just another broken-down drunk like Max.)

"Get me a phone," said Murphy-O'Connor.

A telephone was wheeled into the room. Murphy-O'Connor consulted a memo pad and dialed a number in a distant city. It was Max's hometown. Our receiver was rigged electronically so that the party dialed could be heard loud and clear throughout the living room on the lake.

"Hank Shea?"

"Yeah, who's this?"

"My name is Sean Murphy-O'Connor. I am a counselor at an alcohol and drug rehabilitation center in the Midwest. Do you remember a customer named Max? [Pause.] Good. With his family's permission I am researching his drinking history. You tend bar in that tavern every afternoon, so I am wondering if you could tell me approximately how much Max drinks each day?"

"I know Max well, but are you sure you have his permission to question me?"

"I have a signed affidavit. Shoot."

"He's a heck of a guy. I really like him. He drops thirty bucks in here every afternoon. Max has his standard six martinis, buys a few drinks, and always leaves me a fin. Good man."

Max leapt to his feet. Raising his right hand defiantly, he unleashed a stream of profanity worthy of a stevedore. He attacked Murphy-O'Connor's ancestry, impugned Charlie's legitimacy and the whole unit's integrity. He clawed at the sofa and spat on the rug.

Then, in an incredible *coup de main*, he immediately regained his composure. Max reseated himself and remarked matter-of-factly that even Jesus lost His temper in the temple when he saw the Sadducees hawking pigeons and pastries. After an extemporaneous homily to the group on justifiable anger, he stoved his pipe and presumed that the interrogation was over.

"Have you ever been unkind to one of your kids?" Fred asked.

"Glad you brought that up, Fred. I have a fantastic rapport with my four boys. Last Thanksgiving I took them on a fishing expedition to the Rockies. Four days of roughing it in the wilderness. A great time! Two of my sons graduated from Harvard, you know, and Max Jr. is in his third year at…"

"I didn't ask you that. At least once in his life every father has been unkind to one of his kids. I'm sixty-two years old and I can vouch for it. Now give us one specific example."

A long pause ensued. Finally, "Well, I was a little thoughtless with my nine-year-old daughter last Christmas Eve."

"What happened?"

"I don't remember. I just get this heavy feeling whenever I think about it."

"Where did it happen? What were the circumstances?"

"Wait one minute!" Max's voice rose in anger. "I told you I don't remember. Just can't shake this bad feeling."

Unobtrusively, Murphy-O'Connor dialed Max's hometown once more and spoke with his wife.

"Sean Murphy-O'Connor calling, ma'am. We are in the middle of a group therapy session, and your husband just told us that he was unkind to your daughter last Christmas Eve. Can you give me the details, please?"

A soft voice filled the room. "Yes, I can tell you the whole thing. It seems like it just happened yesterday. Our daughter Debbie wanted a pair of earth shoes for her Christmas present. On the afternoon of December 24, my husband drove her downtown, gave her sixty dollars, and told her to buy the best pair of shoes in the store. That is exactly what she did. When she climbed back into the pickup truck her father was driving, she kissed him on the cheek and told him he was the best daddy in the whole world. Max was preening himself like a peacock and decided to celebrate on the way home. He stopped at the Cork 'n' Bottle—that's a tavern a few miles from our house—and told Debbie he would be right out. It was a clear and extremely cold day, about twelve degrees above zero, so Max left the motor running and locked both doors from the outside so no one could get in. It was a little after three in the afternoon and..."

Silence.

"Yes?"

The sound of heavy breathing crossed the recreation room. Her voice grew faint. She was crying. "My husband met some old Army buddies in the tavern. Swept up in euphoria over the reunion, he lost track of time, purpose, and everything else. He came out of the Cork 'n' Bottle at midnight. He was drunk. The motor had stopped running and the car windows were frozen shut. Debbie was badly frostbitten on both ears and on her fingers. When we got her to the hospital, the doctors had to operate. They amputated the thumb and forefinger on her right hand. She will be deaf for the rest of her life."

Max appeared to be having a coronary. He struggled to his feet making jerky, uncoordinated movements. His glasses flew to the right and his pipe to the left. He collapsed on all fours and sobbed hysterically.

Murphy-O'Connor stood up and said softly, "Let's split."

Twenty-four recovering alcoholics and addicts climbed the eight-step stairwell. We turned left, gathered along the railing on the upper split level and looked down. No man will ever forget what he saw that day, the twenty-fourth of April at exactly high noon. Max was still in the doggy position. His sobs had soared to shrieks. Murphy-O'Connor approached him, pressed his foot against Max's rib cage and pushed. Max rolled over on his back.

"You unspeakable slime," Murphy-O'Connor roared. "There's the door on your right and the window on your left. Take whichever is fastest. Get out of here before I throw up. I am not running a rehab for liars!"

The philosophy of tough love is based on the conviction that no effective recovery can be initiated until a man admits that he is powerless over alcohol and that his life has become unmanageable. The alternative to confronting the truth is always some form of self-destruction. For Max there were three options: eventual insanity, premature death, or sobriety. In order to free the captive, one must name the captivity. Max's denial had to be identified through merciless interaction with his peers. His self-deception had to be unmasked in its absurdity.

Later that same day Max pleaded for and obtained permission to continue treatment. He proceeded to undergo the most striking personality change I have ever witnessed. He got honest and became more open, sincere, vulnerable, and affectionate than any man in the group. Tough love had made him real and the truth had set him free.

The denouement to his story: The night before Max completed treatment, Fred passed by his room. The door was ajar. Max was sitting at his desk reading a novel entitled *Watership Down.* Fred knocked and entered. For several moments Max sat staring at the book. When he looked up, his cheeks were streaked with tears. "Fred," he said hoarsely, "I just prayed for the first time in my life." Max was on the road to knowing God.[1]

An intimate connection exists between the quest for honesty and a transparent personality. Max could not encounter the truth of the living God until he faced his alcoholism. From a biblical perspective, Max was a liar. In philosophy, the opposite of truth is error; in Scripture, the opposite of truth is a lie. Max's lie consisted in appearing to be something he wasn't—a social drinker. Truth for him meant acknowledging reality—his alcoholic drinking.

The Evil One is the great illusionist. He varnishes the truth and encourages dishonesty. "If we say, 'We have no sin,' we are deceiving ourselves, and the truth has no place in us" (1 John 1:8). Satan prompts us to give importance to what has no importance. He clothes trivia with glitter and seduces us away from what is real. He causes us to live in a world of delusion, unreality, and shadows.

Jean Danielou wrote, "Truth consists in the mind giving to things the importance they have in reality." The really Real is God. When Max confronted and accepted the truth of his alcoholism, he stepped through a doorway into the acknowledgment of God's sovereign reality and claimed, "I just prayed for the first time in my life."

The noonday devil of the Christian life is the temptation to lose the inner self while preserving the shell of edifying behavior. Suddenly I discover that I am ministering to AIDS victims to enhance my résumé. I find I renounced ice cream for Lent to lose five excess pounds. I drop hints about the absolute priority of meditation and contemplation to create the impression that I am a man of prayer. At some unremembered moment I have lost the connection between internal purity of heart and external works of piety. In the most humiliating sense of the word, I have become a legalist. I have fallen victim to what T. S. Eliot calls the greatest sin: to do the right thing for the wrong reason.

"Beware of the scribes…these are the men who devour the property of widows and for show offer long prayers" (Mark 12:38–40). Jesus did not have a naive outlook on prayer. He knew it could be counterfeited by spiritual narcissism, hypocrisy, wordiness, and sensationalism. The noonday devil is not intimidated by the boundaries of time.

The letter of James counsels us to confess our sins to one another (James 5:16). This salutary practice aims to guide us in accepting ownership of our ragamuffin status. But as Dietrich Bonhoeffer noted:

> He who is alone with his sins is utterly alone. It may be that Christians, notwithstanding corporate worship, common prayer, and all their fellowship in service, may still be left to their loneliness. The final breakthrough to fellowship does not occur because, though they have fellowship with one another as believers and as devout people, they do not have fellowship as the undevout, as sinners. The pious fellowship permits no one to be a sinner. So everyone must conceal his sin from himself and from their fellowship. We dare not be sinners. Many Christians are unthinkably horrified when a real sinner is suddenly discovered among the righteous. So we remain alone with our sin, living in lies and hypocrisy. The fact is that we are sinners![2]

At Sunday worship, as in every dimension of our existence, many of us *pretend to believe* we are sinners. Consequently, all we can do is pretend to believe we have been forgiven. As a result, our whole spiritual life is pseudo-repentance and pseudo-bliss.

The appeal of paste jewelry and sawdust hot dogs is powerful. A small investment in apparent propriety and good deeds yields the rewards of the faith community—adulation and praise. Coupled with a charismatic personality and an attractive appearance, hypocrisy can earn a $640,000 apartment at Trump Towers, a $90,000 diamond ring from Tiffany's, and frequent flights to Europe.

The spiritual future of ragamuffins consists not in disavowing that we are sinners but in accepting that truth with growing clarity, rejoicing in God's incredible longing to rescue us in spite of everything. C. S. Lewis wrote:

> It may be that salvation consists not in the canceling of these eternal moments but in the perfected humility that bears the shame forever, rejoicing in the occasion which is furnished to God's compassion and glad that it should be common knowledge to the universe. Perhaps in that eternal moment St. Peter—he will forgive me if I am wrong—forever denies his Master. If so, it would indeed be true that the joys of heaven are for most of us, in our present condition, an acquired taste—and certain ways of life may render the taste impossible of acquisition. Perhaps the lost are those who dare not go to such a public place.[3]

Biblically, there is nothing more detestable than a self-righteous disciple. He is so swollen with conceit that his mere presence is unbearable. However, a nagging question arises. Have I so insulated myself in a fortified city of rationalizations that I cannot see that I may not be as different from the self-righteous as I would like to think?

The following scenario plays in my imagination. A humble woman seeks me out because of my vaunted reputation as a spiritual guide. She is simple and direct: "Please teach me how to pray."

Tersely, I inquire, "Tell me about your prayer life."

She lowers her eyes and says contritely, "There's not much to tell. I say grace before meals."

Haughtily, I reply, "You say grace before meals! Isn't that nice, Madam. I say grace upon waking and before retiring, and grace again before reading the newspaper and turning on the television. I say grace before ambulating and meditating, before the theater and the opera, before jogging, swimming, biking, dining, lecturing, and writing. I even say grace before I say grace."

That night, soggy with self-approval, I go before the Lord. And He whispers, "You ungrateful swine. Even the desire to say grace is itself My gift."

There is an ancient Christian legend that goes this way: "When the son of God was nailed to the cross and gave up his spirit, he went straight down to hell from the cross and set free all the sinners who were there in torment. And the devil wept and mourned for he thought he would get no more sinners for hell.

"Then God said to him, 'Do not weep, for I shall send you all those holy people who have become self-complacent in the consciousness of their goodness and self-righteous in their condemnation of sinners. And hell shall be filled up once more for generations until I come again.'"[4]

How long will it be before we discover we cannot dazzle

God with our accomplishments?

When will we acknowledge that we need not and cannot buy God's favor?

When will we acknowledge that we don't have it all together and happily accept the gift of grace? When will we grasp the thrilling truth of Paul, "Someone is reckoned as upright not by practicing the Law but by faith in Jesus Christ" (Galatians 2:16)?

Authentic faith leads us to treat others with unconditional seriousness and to a loving reverence for the mystery of the human personality. Authentic Christianity should lead to maturity, personality, and reality. It should fashion whole men and women living lives of love and communion.

False, manhandled religion produces the opposite effect. Whenever religion shows contempt or disregards the rights of persons, even under the noblest pretexts, it draws us away from reality and God. We can put "reverse English" on religion and make religion an escape from religion.

John's Gospel shows the religious leaders of Israel worried about Jesus:

> The chief priests and Pharisees called a meeting. "Here is this man working all these signs," they said, "and what action are we taking? If we let him go on in this way everybody will believe in him, and the Romans will come and suppress the Holy Place and our nation." One of them, Caiaphas, the high priest that year, said, "You do not seem to have grasped the situation at all; you fail to see that it is to your advantage that one

man should die for the people, rather than that the
whole nation should perish." (John 11:47–50)

A terrible thing has happened to Caiaphas: Religion has left
the realm of respect for person. For Caiaphas, sacredness has
become institutions, structures, and abstractions. He is dedicated to "the people," so individual flesh and blood men are
expendable. Caiaphas is dedicated to the nation. But the nation
does not bleed like Jesus. Caiaphas is dedicated to the Temple—
impersonal brick and mortar. Caiaphas became impersonal
himself, no longer a warm human being but a robot, as fixed
and rigid as his unchanging world.

The choice usually presented to Christians is not
between Jesus and Barabbas. No one wants to appear an
obvious murderer. The choice to be careful about is between
Jesus and Caiaphas. And Caiaphas can fool us. He is a very
"religious" man.

The spirit of Caiaphas lives on in every century of religious
bureaucrats who confidently condemn good people who have
broken bad religious laws. Always for a good reason of course:
for the good of the temple, for the good of the church. How
many sincere people have been banished from the Christian
community by religious power brokers as numb in spirit as
Caiaphas!

The deadening spirit of hypocrisy lives on in prelates and
politicians who want to look good but not be good; it lives on
in people who prefer to surrender control of their souls to rules
rather than run the risk of living in union with Jesus.

Eugene Kennedy writes:

The devil dwells in the urge to control rather than liberate the human soul... We stand by a dark forest through which fearful religious and political leaders would force us to pass in single file through their exclusive pathway of righteousness. They want to intimidate us, make us afraid and hand over our souls to them once more. Jesus saw such shadowed forces as the corrupters of the essential nature of religion in his time. They are no less so all these centuries later.[5]

The way we are with each other is the truest test of our faith. How I treat a brother or sister from day to day, how I react to the sin-scarred wino on the street, how I respond to interruptions from people I dislike, how I deal with normal people in their normal confusion on a normal day may be a better indication of my reverence for life than the antiabortion sticker on the bumper of my car.

We are not pro-life simply because we are warding off death. We are pro-life to the extent that we are men and women for others, all others; to the extent that no human flesh is a stranger to us; to the extent that we can touch the hand of another in love; to the extent that for us there are no "others."

Today the danger of the pro-life position, which I vigorously support, is that it can be frighteningly selective. The rights of the unborn and the dignity of the age-worn are pieces of the same pro-life fabric. We weep at the unjustified destruction of the unborn. Did we also weep when the evening news reported from Arkansas that a black family had been shotgunned out of a white neighborhood?

One morning I experienced a horrifying hour. I tried to remember how often between 1941 and 1988 I wept for a German or Japanese, a North Korean or North Vietnamese, a Sandinista or Cuban. I could not remember one. Then I wept, not for them, but for myself.

When we laud life and blast abortionists, our credibility as Christians is questionable. On one hand we proclaim the love and anguish, the pain and joy that goes into fashioning a single child. We proclaim how precious each life is to God and should be to us. On the other hand, when it is the enemy that shrieks to heaven with his flesh in flames, we do not weep, we are not shamed; we call for more.

The sensitive Jew remembers the Middle Ages—every ghetto structured by Christians, every forced baptism, every Good Friday pogrom, every portrait of Shylock exacting his pound of flesh, every identifying dress or hat or badge, every death for conscience's sake, every back turned or shoulder shrugged, every sneer and slap and curse.

With their tragic history as background, it is not surprising that many Jews are unimpressed with our anti-abortion stance and our arguments for the sacredness of human life. For they still hear cries of "Christ-killer!" The survivors of Auschwitz and Dachau still feel lashes on their backs; they still see images of human soap, still taste hunger, still smell gas. The history of Judaism is a story of caring: They are not sure we care for them.

The pro-life position is a seamless garment of reverence for the unborn and the age-worn, for the enemy, the Jew, and the quality of life of all people. Otherwise, it is paste jewelry and sawdust hot dogs.

Relief comes from rigorous honesty with ourselves. It is interesting that whenever the evangelists Mark, Luke, or John mention the apostles, they call the author of the first Gospel either Levi or Matthew. But in his own Gospel, he always refers to himself as "Matthew the publican," never wanting to forget who he was and always wanting to remember how low Jesus stooped to pick him up.

We are publicans just like Matthew.

Honesty simply asks if we are open, willing, and able to acknowledge this truth. Honesty brings an end to pretense through a candid acknowledgment of our fragile humanity. It is always unpleasant, and usually painful, and that is why I am not very good at it. But to stand in the truth before God and one another has a unique reward. It is the reward which a sense of reality always brings: I know something extremely precious. I am in touch with myself as I am. My tendency to play the pseudo-messiah is torpedoed.

To the extent that I reject my ragamuffin identity, I turn away from God, the community, and myself. I become a man obsessed by illusion, a man of false power and fearful weakness, unable to think, act, or love.

Gerald May, a Christian psychiatrist in Washington DC, writes:

> Honesty before God requires the most fundamental risk
> of faith we can take: the risk that God is good, that God

does love us unconditionally. It is in taking this risk that we rediscover our dignity. To bring the truth of ourselves, just as we are, to God, just as God is, is the most dignified thing we can do in this life.[6]

Lord Jesus, we are silly sheep who have dared to
stand before You and try to bribe You with our
preposterous portfolios. Suddenly we have come to
our senses. We are sorry and ask You to forgive us.
Give us the grace to admit we are ragamuffins,
to embrace our brokenness, to celebrate Your mercy
when we are at our weakest, to rely on Your
mercy no matter what we may do.
Dear Jesus, gift us to stop grandstanding and trying
to get attention, to do the truth quietly without display,
to let the dishonesties in our lives fade away, to accept
our limitations, to cling to the gospel of grace,
and to delight in Your love. Amen.

Chapter Eight

FREEDOM FROM FEAR

In Dostoyevsky's incomparable novel *The Brothers Karamazov,* the charge flung by the Church—embodied in the Grand Inquisitor—against Jesus who has returned to earth is, "Why have you come to disturb us?"

After fifteen hundred years the institutional Church, instead of proclaiming Jesus, had supplanted Him. Ecclesiastical traditions and man-made laws had usurped Jesus, and the Church was living off the success of its ingenuity.

There was too much light and truth in Jesus. His word, "You will know the truth and the truth will make you free," was intolerable. The elders decided that men and women simply were not capable of being free; so the Church ascribed to itself the protection of souls entrusted to it, only to dispense it when absolutely necessary. Ordinary people could not endure the

burden of freedom, so the Church took it away from them for
their own good. They would only abuse and misuse it anyway.
Delivered from the anxiety and torment of personal decision
and responsibility, people would feel safe and happy in obedience to authority.

> "They will be amazed at us," says the Grand Inquisitor
> to Jesus, "and will think of us as gods, because we, who
> set ourselves at their head, are ready to endure freedom,
> this freedom from which they shrink in horror; and
> because we are ready to rule over them—so terrible will
> it seem to them, in the end, to be free. But we shall say
> that we are obeying you and ruling only in your name.
> Again we shall be betraying them, for we shall not let you
> have anything to do with us anymore." Indeed, "Why
> have you come to disturb us?" The Grand Inquisitor
> means to take this Jesus who has come again, bringing
> freedom once again, and burn him at the stake in the
> name of the Church.[1]

The question had become not "What does Jesus say?" but
"What does the Church say?" This question is still being asked
today.

Sad but true: Some Christians want to be slaves. It is easier
to let others make decisions or to rely upon the letter of the law.

Raised from the dead, Jesus remains present in the community of disciples as the way to freedom. The kingdom of
God is a kingdom of freedom. Jesus invites and challenges us to
enter this kingdom, to walk the royal road of freedom, to be set

free by the Father's love. He calls ragamuffins everywhere to freedom from the fear of death, freedom from the fear of life, and freedom from anxiety over our salvation.

One of the loveliest lines I have ever read comes from Brother Roger, the Prior of the Protestant monks of Taize, France: "Assured of your salvation by the unique grace of our Lord Jesus Christ."[2] It is still difficult for me to read these words without tears filling my eyes. It is wonderful. Christ bore my sins, took my place, died for me, freed me from fear to walk the path of peace that leads to the Twelve Gates.

Sadly, many today are not experiencing what Paul calls "the same glorious freedom as the children of God" (Romans 8:21). The basic problem was stated in the first chapter of this book: We accept grace in theory but deny it in practice. Living by grace rather than law leads us out of the house of fear into the house of love. "In love there is no room for fear, but perfect loves drives out fear: because fear implies punishment, and no one who is afraid has come to perfection in love" (1 John 4:18).

While we profess our faith in god's unconditional love, many of us still live in fear. Nouwen remarks:

Look at the many "if" questions we raise: What am I going to do if I do not find a spouse, a house, a job, a friend, a benefactor? What am I going to do if they fire me, if I get sick, if an accident happens, if I lose my friends, if my marriage does not work out, if a war breaks out? What if tomorrow the weather is bad, the buses are on strike, or an earthquake happens? What if someone steals my money, breaks into my house, rapes my daughter, or kills me?[3]

Once these questions guide our lives, we take out a second mortgage in the house of fear.

Jesus says simply, "Make your home in me, as I make mine in you" (John 15:4). Home is not a heavenly mansion in the afterlife but a safe place right in the midst of our anxious world. "Anyone who loves me will keep my word, and my Father will love him, and we shall come to him and make a home in him" (John 14:23).

Home is that sacred space—external or internal—where we don't have to be afraid; where we are confident of hospitality and love. In our society we have many homeless people sleeping not only on the streets, in shelters or in welfare hotels, but vagabonds who are in flight, who never come home to themselves. They seek a safe place through alcohol or drugs or security in success, competence, friends, pleasure, notoriety, knowledge, or even a little religion. They have become strangers to themselves, people who have an address but are never at home, who never hear the voice of love or experience the freedom of God's children.

To those of us in flight, who are afraid to turn around lest we run into ourselves, Jesus says, *You have a home. I am your home. Claim me as your home. You will find it to be the intimate place where I have found my home. It is right where you are, in your innermost being. In your heart.*

The author of Hebrews describes Jesus as the one who has "set free all those who had been held in slavery all their lives by the fear of death" (Hebrews 2:15). The gospel of freedom proclaims that death is an illusion, a phantom, the bogeyman of little children. Death is simply a transition into the one experience worthy of the name *life*.

Here is the root of Christian joy and mirth. It is why theologian Robert Hotchkins at the University of Chicago can insist:

> Christians ought to be celebrating constantly. We ought to be preoccupied with parties, banquets, feasts, and merriment. We ought to give ourselves over to veritable orgies of joy because we have been liberated from the fear of life and the fear of death. We ought to attract people to the church quite literally by the fun there is in being a Christian.

Unfortunately we sometimes become somber, serious, and pompous. We fly in the face of freedom and grimly dig deeper into the trenches. In the words of Teresa of Avila, "From silly devotions and sour-faced saints, spare us, O Lord."

Disgruntled and disgusted, The Prince of Darkness slinks up to the chalet of bummed-out disciples who have made their home in Jesus and nails a legal document to the door:

E V I C T I O N   N O T I C E !

You are hereby banished from
the House of Fear forever.
With malice aforethought, you have
flagrantly withheld the monthly rent
Of guilt, anxiety, fear, shame

and self-condemnation.
You have adamantly refused to
worry about your salvation.
Already I overheard one dismal tenant say,
"There goes the neighborhood!"
Your freedom from fear is not only
dangerous but contagious.
Real estate values have plummeted;
gullible investors are hard to find.
Why? Your callous and carefree
rejection of slavery!
A pox on you and
all deluded lovers of liberty!
The Prince

We must choose either Christ or the Law as author of salvation. Does freedom come through faith in Jesus or through
obedience to the Torah? The issue is momentous. "Christ set us
free, so that we should remain free. Stand firm, then, and do
not let yourselves be fastened again to the yoke of slavery"
(Galatians 5:1). Jewish Christians were proclaiming that salvation was impossible without observance of the Mosaic Law.
They promoted not simply supererogatory practices (acts
beyond what faith calls for) but another gospel, which distorts
the gospel of Christ (Galatians 1:6–7).

Paul is livid in his epistle to the Galatians: "You stupid
people in Galatia!" (3:1). What hangs in the balance is the
emancipation of Christianity. Paul is uncompromising: "We
too came to believe in Christ Jesus so as to be reckoned as

upright by faith in Christ and not by practicing the Law: since no human being can be found upright by keeping the Law" (2:16). "Now it is obvious that nobody is reckoned as upright in God's sight by the Law, since the upright will live through faith" (3:11). "Christ redeemed us from the curse of the Law by being cursed for our sake" (3:13).

Written in the heat of the moment, the letter is a flaming manifesto of Christian freedom. Christ's call on our lives is a call to liberty. Freedom is the cornerstone of Christianity. Would Paul be as apoplectic today at the goings-on in the American church? "I am astonished that you are so promptly turning away from the one who called you in the grace of Christ and are going over to a different gospel" (1:6). Would those still imprisoned in old guilts, crippled by fear, exhausted by scrupulosity, threatened by legalists, and anxious over their salvation merit the same rebuke?

We have undoubtedly heard that freedom is not a license for lust. Maybe that's all we've heard—what it *isn't*.

Such an approach, whatever its limited truth, is defensive and afraid. Those using it wish above all to warn us of the dangers of thinking about freedom, of yearning for freedom. Such an approach generally ends up by showing us, or at least attempting to show us, that freedom actually consists in following the law or in submitting to authority or in walking a well-trod path. Again, there may be some truth in these conclusions, but there is lacking a sense of the dark side of law, and of authority, and of the well-trod path. Each may be and has been turned into an instrument of tyranny and human suffering.[4]

What does freedom in the Spirit look like? "Now this Lord is the Spirit and where the Spirit of the Lord is, there is freedom" (2 Corinthians 3:17).

Freedom in Christ produces a healthy independence from peer pressure, people-pleasing, and the bondage of human respect. The tyranny of public opinion can manipulate our lives. *What will the neighbors think? What will my friends think?* The expectations of others can exert a subtle but controlling pressure on our behavior.

As the chameleon changes colors with the seasons, so the Christian who wants to be well thought of by everyone attunes and adapts to each new personality and situation. Without a stable and enduring self-image, a woman may offer radically different aspects of herself to different men; she may be pious with her pastor and seductive with the office manager. Depending upon company and circumstances, a man may be either a sweet-talking servant of God or a foulmouthed, bottom-pinching boor. Continuity of character is conspicuously absent in both sexes.

"It seems only yesterday that we began to break out of our character armor," writes William Kilpatrick, "only a moment ago that we began to experiment with a wide range of possibilities, identities, and relationships. Swings of the pendulum, however, take place rather rapidly these days . . . and already the pendulum of identity formation has taken an exaggerated swing toward fluidity and tentativeness and away from continuity and fidelity."[5]

In Christ Jesus freedom from fear empowers us to let go

of the desire to appear good, so that we can move freely in the mystery of who we really are. Preoccupation with projecting the "nice guy" image, impressing newcomers with our experience, and relying heavily on the regard of others leads to self-consciousness, sticky pedestal behavior, and unfreedom in the iron grip of human respect. Unconsciously, we may clothe the Pharisee's prayer in the publican's formula. For most of us it takes a long time for the Spirit of freedom to cleanse us of the subtle urges to be admired for our studied goodness. It requires a strong sense of our redeemed selves to pass up the opportunity to appear graceful and good to other persons.

Alms-giving affords such an opportunity, but the applause we hear will be payment in full for our generous offering. Self-consciousness, not virtue, is its own reward.

> But who can escape watching oneself do good in a world in which even the churches that worship Jesus have mastered the techniques of embarrassing people into charitable giving? How can free giving, blind as Justice balancing the scales, survive the pastor's printed list of donors, the intricacies of charity for tax purposes, booster ads, and testimonial tickets wheedled out of us with the sly pressures of shame and guilt? Our fundraising mechanisms are built on an appraisal of our motives that is as clear and uncluttered as that of Jesus; they are engineered to our hearts like bionic devices and they reveal a mixed rather than a totally crass picture of our impulses for giving.[6]

The account of the widow's mite suggests that all the best gifts come from the loving hearts of men and women who aren't trying to impress anybody, even themselves, and who have won freedom precisely because they have stopped trying to trap life into paying them back for the good they do.

I experienced a significant breakthrough into the freedom of the children of God at my first AA meeting. In the past I would have set great store not only on looking good but on thinking too often about who is looking. My self-image as a man of God and a disciplined disciple had to be protected at all costs. My ravenous insecurities made my sense of self-worth rise and fall like a sailboat on the winds of another's approval or disapproval. It was a supreme moment of liberation to stand up, kick the pedestal aside, and simply state, "My name is Brennan. I am an alcoholic."

My spiritual director once told me, "Brennan, give up trying to look and sound like a saint. It will be a lot easier on everybody."

Living by grace inspires a growing consciousness that I am what I am in the sight of Jesus and nothing more. It is His approval that counts. Making our home in Jesus, as He makes His in us, leads to creative listening: *Has it crossed your mind that I am proud you accepted the gift of faith I offered you? Proud that you freely chose Me, after I had chosen you, as your friend and Lord? Proud that, with all your warts and wrinkles, you haven't given up? Proud that you believe in Me enough to try again and again? Are you aware how I appreciate you for wanting Me? I want you to know how grateful I am when you pause to smile and comfort a child who has lost her way. I am grateful for the hours*

you devote to learning more about Me; for the word of encourage-
ment you passed on to your burnt-out pastor; for your visit to the
shut-in; for your tears for the retarded. What you did to them, you
did to Me. Alas, I am sad when you do not believe that I have
totally forgiven you or you feel uncomfortable approaching Me.

Prayer is another area that many struggle with because they aren't aware that in the freedom of the Spirit there are as many ways of praying as there are individual believers. The cardinal rule in prayer remains the dictum of Don Chapman: "Pray as you can; don't pray as you can't."

Let us suppose you give your three-year-old daughter a coloring book and a box of crayons for her birthday. The following day, with the proud smile only a little one can muster, she presents her first pictures for inspection. She has colored the sun black, the grass purple, and the sky green. In the lower right-hand corner, she has added woozy wonders of floating slabs and hovering rings; on the left, a panoply of colorful, carefree squiggles. You marvel at her bold strokes and intuit that her psyche is railing against its own cosmic puniness in the face of a big, ugly world. Later at the office, you share with your staff your daughter's first artistic effort and you make veiled references to the early work of van Gogh. A little child cannot do a bad coloring; nor can a child of God do bad prayer.

A father is delighted when his little one, leaving off her toys and friends, runs to him and climbs into his arms. As he holds his little one close to him, he cares little whether the child is looking around, her attention flitting from one thing to another, or just settling down to sleep. Essentially the child is choosing to be with her father, confident of the love, the care, the security that is hers in those arms. Our prayer is much like that. We settle down in our Father's arms, in his loving hands. Our mind, our thoughts, our imagination may flit about here and there; we might even fall asleep; but essentially we are choosing for this time to remain intimately with our Father, giving ourselves to him, receiving his love and care, letting him enjoy us as he will. It is very simple prayer. It is very childlike prayer. It is prayer that opens us out to all the delights of the kingdom.[7]

Jesus' tenderness is not in any way determined by how we pray or what we are or do. In order to free us for compassion toward others, Jesus calls us to accept His compassion in our own lives; to become gentle, caring, compassionate, and forgiving toward ourselves in our failure and need.

Compassion for others is not a simple virtue because it avoids snap judgments of right or wrong, good or bad, hero or villain: It seeks truth in all its complexity. Genuine compassion means that in empathizing with the failed plans and uncertain loves of the other person, we send out the vibration, "Yes, ragamuffin, I understand. I've been there, too."

The story goes that a dynamic young businesswoman showed signs of stress and strain. Her doctor prescribed tranquilizers and asked her to report to him after a couple of weeks.

When she came back, he asked her if she felt any different. She said, "No, I don't. But I've observed that other people seem a lot more relaxed."

Usually we see other people not as they are, but as we are.[8]

A person, in a real sense, is what he or she sees. And seeing depends on our eyes. Jesus uses the metaphor of eyes more often than that of the mind or the will. The old proverb, "The eyes are the windows of the soul," contains a profound truth. Our eyes reveal whether our souls are spacious or cramped, hospitable or critical, compassionate or judgmental. The way we see other people is usually the way we see ourselves. If we have made peace with our flawed humanity and embraced our ragamuffin identity, we are able to tolerate in others what was previously unacceptable in ourselves.

One night a seemingly self-absorbed young man arrived at the door to escort our daughter Simone on a date. While he waited in the den for Simone to complete her ablutions, he strutted in the den, affected several poses, muttered some monosyllabic inanities, obliquely studied himself in the mirror, yawned occasionally, and tried to exude a jaunty air of nonchalance. I asked myself, *Who is this young Turk?*

Was he the narcissistic embodiment of smug fulfillment or a touching incarnation of the isolation and loneliness of young people who have been denied access to their own spiritual depths? Behind the mask of studied poses and minor vanities, was there a yearning awaiting redemption?

Judgment depends on what we see, how deeply we look at the other, how honestly we face ourselves, how willing we are to read the human story beneath the frightened face.

The gentleness of Jesus with sinners flowed from His ability to read their hearts. Behind people's grumpiest poses and most puzzling defense mechanisms, behind their arrogance and airs, behind their silence, sneers, and causes, Jesus saw little children who hadn't been loved enough and who had ceased growing because someone had ceased believing in them. His extraordinary sensitivity caused Jesus to speak of the faithful as children, no matter how tall, rich, clever, and successful they might be.

"Assured of your salvation by the unique grace of our Lord Jesus Christ" is the heartbeat of the gospel, joyful liberation from fear of the Final Outcome, a summons to self-acceptance, and freedom for a life of compassion toward others.

Obviously, we are not treating a trivial evangelical matter here. Compassionate love is the axis of the Christian moral revolution and the only sign ever given by Jesus by which a disciple would be recognized: "I give you a new commandment: love one another; you must love one another just as I have loved you. It is by your love for one another, that everyone will recognize you as my disciples" (John 13:34–35). The new commandment structures the new Covenant in the blood of Jesus. So central is the precept of fraternal love that Paul does not hesitate to call it the fulfillment of the entire law and the prophets (see Romans 13:8–10).

Exaggeration and overstatement are not the danger here. The danger lurks in our subtle attempts to rationalize our moderation in this regard. Turning the other cheek, walking the extra mile, offering no resistance to injury, and forgiving seventy times seven are not whims of the Son of Man. The only thing that matters is "faith working through love" (Galatians 5:6).

"Reason demands moderation in love as in all things," writes John McKenzie, "but faith destroys moderation here.

Faith tolerates a moderate love of one's fellow man no more than it tolerates a moderate love between God and man."[9]

Once again, gentleness toward ourselves constitutes the core of our gentleness with others. When the compassion of Christ is interiorized and appropriated to self—"He will not break the crushed reed, or snuff the faltering wick" (Matthew 12:20)—the breakthrough into a compassionate stance toward others occurs. In a catch-22 situation, the way of gentleness brings healing to ourselves and gentleness toward ourselves brings healing to others. Solidarity with ragamuffins frees the one who receives compassion and liberates the one who gives it in the conscious awareness, "I am the other."

Certainly "tough love" and discipline have their place in the Christian family. If children are not educated to the difference between right and wrong, they can easily become neurotic. However, only the discipline administered out of love is corrective and productive. Discipline erupting from rage and vindictiveness is divisive in the family and counterproductive in the church. To present an ultimatum to an addicted teenager, "Seek treatment or split," is a loving and perhaps lifesaving response, as long as the clear distinction between the action and the agent is maintained. With great wisdom William Shakespeare wrote, "Sometimes 'tis necessary to be cruel in order to be kind."

Alcoholics Anonymous was founded on June 10, 1935, in Akron, Ohio, by Bill W. and Doctor Bob. In the organization's early stages a lively debate arose over the qualifications for membership. Could certain individuals be excluded for whatever reason, like some country clubs do? Who gets in and who gets left out? Who decides whether a particular alcoholic is deserving or undeserving? Some of the core group lobbied to limit membership to persons of moral responsibility; others insisted that the only due was the simple admission, "I think I'm an alcoholic, and I want to stop drinking."

According to *Twelve Steps and Twelve Traditions,* whose author naturally remains anonymous, the debate was resolved in a most unusual way. On the AA calendar it was Year Two. In that time nothing could be seen but two nameless, struggling groups of alcoholics trying to hold their faces up to the light.

A newcomer appeared at one of these groups, knocked on the door, and asked to be let in. He talked frankly with the group's oldest member and quickly established that he was a desperate case. Above all, he wanted to get well. "I must tell you that I am the victim of another addiction with a stigmatism even worse than alcoholism. You may not want me among you. Will you let me join your group or not?"

There was the dilemma. What should the group do? The oldest member summoned two others and, in confidence, laid the explosive facts on their laps. Said he, "Well, what about it? If we turn this man away, he'll soon die. If we let him in, only God knows what trouble he'll brew. What's your answer—yes or no?"

At first the elders could only look at the objections. "We deal with alcoholics only," they said. "Should we not sacrifice this one for the sake of the many?" So went the discussion while the newcomer's fate hung in the balance.

Then one of the three spoke in a very different tone. "What we are really afraid of," he said, "is our reputation. We are much more afraid of what people might say than the trouble this alcoholic might bring. As we've been talking, five short words have been running through my mind. Something keeps repeating to me, 'What would the Master do?'"

Not another word was said.

Let's return for a moment to *The Brothers Karamazov*, which hurls a tremendous accusation against the Catholic Church. On innumerable occasions it has sinned against the freedom of the children of God, "but to be honest the accusation does not stand only against the Catholic Church. Or were not heretics and witches burnt at the stake in Calvin's and Luther's Churches too, and were not opponents fought with violence instead of compelled by love. Does not everything of which the Catholic Church is accused in the way of lack of freedom, arbitrariness, authoritarianism, and totalitarianism, exist in other shapes and forms, more or less disguised, among the Christians of other confessions, and indeed often more in small sects than in large churches?"[10]

Yet none of this is decisive. The decisive thing is the freedom of the gospel of Jesus Christ. The ground and source of our freedom lies not in ourselves, who are by nature slaves to sin, *but in the freedom* of His grace setting us free in Christ by the Holy Spirit. We are free from the slavery of sin—for what? For the saving grace of the living God!

The Grand Inquisitor, an old man with withered face and sunken eyes, finally ended his blistering indictment against Jesus' naiveté and idealism.

When the Inquisitor ceased speaking, he waited some

time for his Prisoner to answer him. His silence weighed down upon him. He saw that the Prisoner had listened intently all the time, looking gently in his face and evidently not wishing to reply. The old man longed for Him to say something, however bitter and terrible. But He suddenly approached the old man in silence and softly kissed him on his bloodless aged lips. That was all His answer. The old man shuddered. His lips moved. He went to the door, opened it, and said to Him, "Go..."[11]

And the kiss glowed in the old man's heart.

Chapter Nine

†HE SECOND CALL

*M*any people between the ages of thirty and sixty—whatever their stature in the community and whatever their personal achievements—undergo what can truly be called a second journey.

A man can have piled up an impressive portfolio of dollars and honors, get his name in *Who's Who,* and then wake up one morning asking, "Is it all worth it?" Competent teachers, nurses, and clergy can reach the top only to discover that the job no longer fascinates; there is nowhere higher to go. They find themselves terrified of stagnation and asking, "Should I switch careers? Would returning to school help?"

Gail Sheehy's second journey began at thirty-five when she was covering a story in northern Ireland. She was standing next to a young man when a bullet blew off his face. On that Bloody

Sunday in Londonderry, she felt herself confronted with death and with what she called "the arithmetic of life." She suddenly realized, "No one is with me. No one keeps me safe. There is no one who won't ever leave me alone." Bloody Sunday threw Gail Sheehy off balance and flung at her a barrage of painful questions about her ultimate purpose and values.

It need not be a bullet that initiates a second journey. A thirty-five-year-old wife learns of her husband's infidelity. A forty-year-old company director finds that making money suddenly seems absurd. A forty-five-year-old journalist gets smashed up in a car accident. However it happens, such people feel confused and even lost. They can no longer keep life in working order. They are dragged away from chosen and cherished patterns to face strange crises. This is their second journey.[1]

Anne Tyler's heroine in her Pulitzer Prize–winning novel, *Breathing Lessons,* is driving along a country road with her husband at the wheel. Suddenly, this middle-aged woman cries out, "O Ira, what are we going to do with the rest of our lives?" This is the question of the second journey.

Second journeys usually end quietly with a new wisdom and a coming to a true sense of self that releases great power. The wisdom is that of an adult who has regained equilibrium, stabilized, and found fresh purpose and new dreams. It is a wisdom that gives some things up, lets some things die, and accepts human limitations. It is a wisdom that realizes: *I cannot expect anyone to understand me fully.* It is wisdom that admits the inevitability of old age and death. It is a wisdom that has faced the pain caused by parents, spouse, family, friends, colleagues, business associates, and has truly forgiven them and acknowledged with unexpected compassion that these people are neither angels nor devils, but only human.

The second journey begins when we know we cannot live the afternoon of life according to the morning program. We are aware that we only have a limited amount of time left to accomplish that which is really important—and that awareness illumines for us what really matters, what really counts. This conviction provides a new center. We share the determination of John Henry Newman who, as his second journey comes to a close, heads home, sensing, "I have a work to do in England."[2]

For the Christian, this second journey usually occurs between the ages of thirty and sixty and is often accompanied by a second call from the Lord Jesus. The second call invites us to serious reflection on the nature and quality of our faith in the gospel of grace, our hope in the new and not yet, and our love for God and people. The second call is a summons to a deeper, more mature commitment of faith where the naiveté, first fervor, and untested idealism of the morning and the first commitment have been seasoned with pain, rejection, failure, loneliness, and self-knowledge.

The call asks, *Do you really accept the message that God is head over heels in love with you?* I believe that this question is at the core of our ability to mature and grow spiritually. If in our hearts we really don't believe that God loves us as we are, if we are still tainted by the lie that we can do something to make God love us more, we are rejecting the message of the cross.

What stands in the way of our embracing the second call?

I can see three obstacles: a crisis of faith, of hope, and of love. Let me explain.

Imagine that Jesus is calling you today. He extends a second invitation—to accept His Father's love. And maybe you answer, "Oh, I know that. It's old hat. I've come to this book seeking an insight in a fit of fervor. I'm wide open. I'll listen to anything you have to say, so go ahead, dazzle me. Lay a new word on me. I know the old one."

And God answers, *That's what you don't know. You don't know how much I love you. The moment you think you understand is the moment you do not understand. I am God, not man. You tell others about Me—that I am a loving God. Your words are glib. My words are written in the blood of My only Son. The next time you preach about My love with such obnoxious familiarity, I may come and blow your whole prayer meeting apart. When you come at Me with studied professionalism, I will expose you as a rank amateur. When you try to convince others that you understand what you are talking about, I will tell you to shut up and fall flat on your face. You claim you know I love you.*

Did you know that every time you tell Me you love Me, I say thank you?

When your son comes to you asking, "Do you like Susan more 'cause she skates better and she's a girl?" are you grieved and saddened over your child's lack of trust? Do you know that you do the same thing to Me?

Do you claim to know what we shared when Jesus withdrew to a deserted place or spent the night on a hillside alone with Me? Do you know from where the inspiration to wash the feet of the Twelve came? Do you understand that, motivated by love alone, your God became your slave in the Upper Room?

Were you grieved by the divine command to Abraham that he slay his only begotten Isaac on Mount Moriah? Were you relieved when the angel intervened, Abraham's hand was stayed, and the sacrifice was not carried out? Have you forgotten that on Good Friday no angel intervened? That sacrifice was carried out, and it was My heart that was broken.

Are you aware that I had to raise Jesus from the dead on Easter morning because My love is everlasting? Are you serenely confident that I will raise you, too, My adopted child?

Faith means you want God and want to want nothing else.

When God's love is taken for granted, we paint Him into a corner and rob Him of the opportunity to love us in a NEW AND SURPRISING way, and faith begins to shrivel and shrink. When I become so spiritually advanced that Abba is old hat, then the Father has been had, Jesus has been tamed, the Spirit has been corralled, and the Pentecostal fire has been extinguished. Evangelical faith is the antithesis of lukewarmness: It always means a profound dissatisfaction with our present state.

In faith there is movement and development. Each day something is new. To be Christian, *faith has to be new*—that is, alive and growing. It cannot be static, finished, settled. When Scripture, prayer, worship, ministry become routine, they are dead. When I conclude that I can now cope with the awful love of God, I have headed for the shallows to avoid the deeps. I could more easily contain Niagara Falls in a teacup than I can comprehend the wild, uncontainable love of God.

If our faith is going to be criticized, let it be for the right reasons. Not because we are too emotional but because we are not emotional enough; not because our passions are so powerful but because they are so puny; not because we are too affectionate but because we lack a deep, passionate, uncompromising affection for Jesus Christ.

Several years ago I made a thirty-day silent retreat in the snow-covered hills of Pennsylvania. One word sounded and resounded in my heart throughout that month. Jesus did not say this on Calvary, though He could have, but He is saying it now: *I'm dying to be with you. I'm really dying to be with you.* It was as if He were calling to me for a second time. I realized that what I thought I knew was straw. I had scarcely glimpsed, I had never dreamed what His love could be. The Lord drove me deeper into solitude seeking not tongues, healing, prophecy, or a good religious experience each time I prayed, but *understanding* and the quest for pure, passionate Presence.

The second call is drawing us to a deeper faith. We need to ask ourselves: *Do I really believe the Good News of Jesus Christ? Do I hear His word spoken to my heart: "Shalom, be at peace, I understand"?* And what is my response to His second call, whispering to me, "You have My love. You don't have to pay for it. You didn't earn it and can't deserve it. You only have to open to it and receive it. You only have to say yes to My love—a love beyond anything you can intellectualize or imagine"?

A second obstacle, closely related to a crisis in faith, is a crisis of hope. In Matthew 22, Jesus describes the kingdom of God as a wedding feast. Do we really believe we are going to a wedding feast that has already begun? Are we optimistic about what will happen to us in this world, or are we fearful and pessimistic? Are we celebrating our union with the Bridegroom?

One evening last summer I was vacationing at the Jersey Shore. I took a walk around an artificial lake in Belmar. Across the lake was a banquet hall called the Barclay that hosted parties, conventions, wedding receptions, and so forth. Over a hundred people were filing in the front door. They had just come from a wedding at St. Rose Church and were going to the reception, which had already begun. They could hear the music and laughter, drinking, and dancing. And the looks on their faces! They were bursting with impatience, sure of their reserved seats, couldn't wait to get in. They looked like they were going to a festive celebration.

But most of us stand outside the banquet door, listening to the merriment and festivity inside, half hoping that there really *is* a banquet in there and that it's the nature of the world to be a celebration. We'd like to go in and celebrate, but wow! What if it's wrong? What if there is no banquet in there? What if it's a trick?

Why don't a lot of us go in now? Because we know that inside it's not a perfect banquet for the simple fact that we are still living between the cross and the resurrection. Christianity doesn't deny the reality of suffering and evil. Remember after Jesus came down the mount of Transfiguration, He told His disciples that He was going up to Jerusalem—that He would be executed and that He would triumph over death. Jesus was not the least bit confident that He would be spared suffering. He knew that suffering was necessary. What He was confident of was vindication. Our hope, our acceptance of the invitation to the banquet, is not based on the idea that we are going to be free of pain and suffering. Rather, it is based on the conviction that we will triumph over suffering.

Do you believe that you, too, will live? Because that's the meaning of Christian hope. It's not a Pollyanna optimism. It's not something that yields to discouragement, defeat, and frustration. On the contrary, Christian hope stands firm and serene, confident even in the face of the gas chamber, even in the face of terminal cancer. However serious we believe Good Friday is, we are confident that Easter Sunday lies ahead of us. And what if we do die? Jesus died, too, and if Jesus died we believe that now He lives and that we shall live, too.

Or do we? Many laypeople have remarked to me that from priests and ministers today they hear just about everything but proclamation of the Good News of the kingdom. They hear about race, pollution, war, abortion, ecology, and myriad other moral problems. None of them prevents proclamation, but not a single one is an adequate substitute for issuing invitations to the banquet. Are we hesitant to commit ourselves to the role of an eschatological herald because we're no longer sure that we believe in that role—another way of saying that we never really did believe it? Maybe we think such a role isn't relevant, that people won't take an eschatological herald seriously. To really be a disciple of Jesus, one must be as committed to the message of the kingdom as He was, and to preach it whether or not the audience finds it relevant.

This is the challenge inherent in the New Testament. If Jesus is to be believed, if His message is to be taken seriously, if God has indeed intervened with loving and saving mercy, then the message is supremely relevant and the issuance of invitations to the wedding banquet is supremely important. But the fundamental issue is not whether the world considers it relevant; it's whether it is true. And this can be decided only by a leap of commitment. One cannot be a disciple without being committed, and if there are many hesitant disciples today, the reason is that they have not yet made a decisive commitment.

This is what the second call of Jesus Christ means today: a summons to a new and more radical leap in hope, to an existential commitment to the Good News of the wedding feast.

If we believe in the exciting message of Jesus, if we hope in vindication, we must love and, even more, we must run the risk of being loved. Love is the third obstacle to our embracing the second call.

The idea that God is love is certainly not new with Jesus. In fact, it probably wasn't even exclusive to the Judeo-Christian tradition. Other men at other times in other parts of the world have thought or hoped or wished that the really REAL, the living God, might actually love them. But Jesus added a note of confidence. He didn't say that *maybe* God was love, or that it would be nice if God were love. He said, GOD IS LOVE—*period.* But there is more to the message of Jesus. He insisted that His Father is crazy with love, that God is a kooky God who can scarcely bear to be without us. The parable that makes this truth so obvious is the story of the prodigal son, the parable of the loving Father.

The emphasis of Christ's story is not on the sinfulness of the son but on the generosity of the Father. We ought to reread this parable periodically if only to catch the delicate nuance at the first meeting between the two. The son had his speech carefully rehearsed; it was an elegant, polished statement of sorrow. But the old man didn't let him finish. The son had barely arrived on the scene when, suddenly, a fine new robe was thrown over his shoulders. He hears music, the fatted calf is being carried into the parlor, and he doesn't even have a chance to say to his father, "I'm sorry."

God wants us back even more than we could possibly want to be back. We don't have to go into great detail about our sorrow. All we have to do, the parable says, is appear on the scene, and before we get a chance to run away again, the Father grabs us and pulls us into the banquet so we can't get away.

There is a fascinating passage in chapter 8 of John's Gospel about the woman caught in sin. Remember how the crowd dragged her before Jesus and asked, "What do we do about her? She was caught in adultery. Moses says we should stone her, but the Romans won't let us stone people. What do *You* think?"

Jesus ignores them and begins to write in the sand. Then He looks up and says, "Well, let the one here who hasn't committed any sin throw the first rock." One by one they drift away. Then Jesus says to the woman, "Is there no one here to condemn you?"

She says, "No one, Lord."

He says, "Okay, go, and don't commit this sin anymore."

Get the picture? Jesus didn't ask her if she was sorry. He didn't demand a firm purpose of amendment. He didn't seem too concerned that she might dash back into the arms of her lover. She just stood there and Jesus gave her absolution before she asked for it.

The nature of God's love for us is outrageous. Why doesn't

this God of ours display some taste and discretion in dealing with us? Why doesn't He show more restraint? To be blunt about it, couldn't God arrange to have a little more dignity? Wow!

Now, if we were in His position, we'd know perfectly well how to behave—that prodigal son would have recited his speech down to the very last word. And when he finished we would have said, "Well, you go away, prodigal son, and I'll think about this a couple of weeks. Then you'll be informed by parcel post whether I've decided to let you back on the farm or not."

I don't think anyone reading this would have approved of throwing rocks at the poor woman in adultery, but we would have made darn sure she presented a detailed act of contrition and was firm in her purpose of amendment. Because if we let her off without saying she was sorry, wouldn't she be back into adultery before sunset?

No, the love of our God isn't dignified at all, and apparently that's the way He expects our love to be. Not only does He require that we accept His inexplicable, embarrassing kind of love; but once we've accepted it, He expects us to behave the same way with others. I suppose I could live, if I had to, with a God whose love for us is embarrassing, but the thought that I've got to act that way with other people—that's a bit too much to swallow.

Perhaps the simplest, though certainly not the easiest, place to start is with myself. Carl Jung, the great psychiatrist, once reflected that we are all familiar with the words of Jesus, "Whatever you do to the least of my brethren, that you do unto me." Then Jung asks a probing question: "What if you discovered that the least of the brethren of Jesus, the one who needs your love the most, the one you can help the most by loving, the one to whom your love will be most meaningful—what if you discovered that this least of the brethren of Jesus…is *you?*"

Then do for yourself what you would do for others. And that wholesome self-love that Jesus enjoined when He said, "Love your neighbor as yourself" might begin with the simple acknowledgment, *What is the story of my priesthood? It is the story of an unfaithful person through whom God continues to work!* That word is not only consoling, it is freeing, especially for those of us caught up in the oppression of thinking that God can only work through saints. What a word of healing, forgiveness, and comfort it is for many of us Christians who have discovered that we are earthen vessels who fulfill Jesus' prophecy, "I tell you solemnly, this day, this night, before the cock crows twice, you will have disowned me three times"!

And the Lord is now calling me a second time, affirming me, enabling me, encouraging me, challenging me all the way into fullness of faith, hope, and love in the power of His Holy Spirit. Ignorant, weak, sinful person that I am, with easy rationalizations for my sinful behavior, I am being told anew in the unmistakable language of love, *I am with you. I am for you. I am in you. I expect more failure from you than you expect from yourself.*

There is one barrier to love that deserves special mention because it is so crucial to the second call of Jesus Christ—fear. Most of us spend considerable time putting off the things we should be doing or we would like to do or we want to do, but are afraid to do. We are afraid of failure. We don't like it, we shun it, we avoid it because of our inordinate desire to be thought well of by others. So we come up with a thousand brilliant excuses for doing nothing. We put things off, waste the energies of life and love that are within us. And the judgment of the Lord High Executioner in *The Mikado* on the girl who perpetually procrastinated falls on us: "She'll never be missed; no, she'll never be missed!"

Each of us pays a heavy price for our fear of falling flat on our faces. It assures the progressive narrowing of our personalities and prevents exploration and experimentation. As we get older we do only the things we do well. There is no growth in Christ Jesus without some difficulty and fumbling. If we are going to keep on growing, we must keep on risking failure throughout our lives. When Max Planck was awarded the Nobel Prize for his discovery of quantum theory, he said, "Looking back over the long and labyrinthine path which finally led to the discovery, I am vividly reminded of Goethe's saying that men will always be making mistakes as long as they are striving after something."

You know, in spite of the fact that Christianity speaks of the cross, redemption, and sin, we're unwilling to admit failure in our own lives. Why? Partly because it's human nature's defense mechanism against its own inadequacies. But even more so, it's because of the successful image our culture demands of us. There are some real problems with projecting the perfect image. First of all, it's simply not true—we are not always happy, optimistic, in command. Second, projecting the flawless image keeps us from reaching people who feel we just wouldn't understand them. And third, even if we could live a life with no conflict, suffering, or mistakes, it would be a shallow existence. The Christian with depth is the person who has failed and who has learned to live with it.

Procrastination is perhaps the worst, most damaging failure of all. We who believe in Jesus, who hope in vindication, who proclaim the love of the heavenly Father, waste our time trying to avoid the things that are most important. How much faith, how much hope, how much love does the perpetual procrastinator really have?[3]

As you go through life, if you acquire any self-awareness, any kind of honest insight into your own personality, you know pretty well what your weaknesses are. You know how you are going to evade the responsibility of faith, hope, and love that Jesus offers. If you're honest, you know that you can't scapegoat, that you can't say it was somebody else's fault. You know that when it comes time for rendering an account of your life, you will be blamed or praised not for what the Pope has done, not for what the bishop has done, not for what the pastor has done (unless you are the pastor). All of us will be blamed or praised according to whether we have accepted the invitation to believe the message.

In the final analysis, the real challenge of Christian growth is the challenge of personal responsibility. The Spirit of Jesus calls out a second time: *Are you going to take charge of your life today? Are you going to be responsible for what you do? Are you going to believe?*

Perhaps we are all in the position of the man in Morton Kelsey's story who came to the edge of an abyss. As he stood there, wondering what to do next, he was amazed to discover a tightrope stretched across the abyss. And slowly, surely, across the rope came an acrobat pushing before him a wheelbarrow with another performer in it. When they finally reached the safety of solid ground, the acrobat smiled at the man's amazement. "Don't you think I can do it again?" he asked.

And the man replied, "Why yes, I certainly believe you can."

The acrobat put his question again, and when the answer was the same, he pointed to the wheelbarrow and said, "Good! Then get in and I will take you across."

What did the traveler do? This is just the question we have to ask ourselves about Jesus Christ. Do we state our belief in Him in no uncertain terms, even in finely articulated creeds, and then refuse to get into the wheelbarrow? What we do about the lordship of Jesus is a better indication of our faith than what we think. This is what the world wants from our rhetoric, what the man of God longs for in a shepherd—someone daring enough to be different, humble enough to make mistakes, wild enough to be burned in the fire of love, real enough to make others see how phony we are.

Let the prayer of Nikos Kazantzakis arise from our hearts at a passionate pitch of loving awareness:

I am a bow on your hands, Lord.
Draw me, lest I rot.
Do not overdraw me, Lord. I shall break.
Overdraw me, Lord, and who cares if I break?[4]

Chapter Ten

THE VICTORIOUS LIMP

The joyous tumult from the Mount Zion Temple Fellowship thundered through the neighborhood. "Amen, brother! Preach it! Tell it like it is!" Rev. Moses Mowinkle was under the anointing. His melodious baritone soared to the heavens, mellowed into the bleating of a lamb, and finally faded to a whisper. As his sermon ended, two hundred worshipers erupted into praise, dancing, weeping, and unrestrained joy. The three-hour worship service ended at noon and the faith community filed out of the church. They all lived on Lemmon Street, the black ghetto.

It was Baltimore in 1938. Racism was deeply implanted in the city. Blacks were considered separate but unequal.

They were tolerated as long as they knew their "place" and stayed in it. The superiority of the white man was universally acknowledged, as was the inferiority of the black man. If some uppity black lost his senses and ventured into an upscale haberdashery in the white part of town, he was not allowed to try on the garments before his possible purchase. After all, a white customer might arrive later and don the same jacket.

The blacks lived in dilapidated shanties: The windows on the second floor offered a splendid view of the white man's garbage cans. For the most part, the Mount Zion Temple Fellowship kept to themselves.

Meanwhile, the raging theological debate uptown was, *How could God have allowed the black Joe Louis to become the heavyweight champion of the world?* Was God exacting vengeance on white people for some unrepented sin? Was it simply the cruel hoax of a whimsical Deity? Or as Woody Allen would put it years later, "If it turns out that there is a God...the worst you can say about Him is that He is, basically, an underachiever.",

Could it be there is no God?

Faith had been restored in 1936 when the Great White Hope from Nazi Germany, Max Schmeling, battered Louis mercilessly for eleven rounds and then floored him with a KO punch in the twelfth. God's honor was vindicated and white supremacy restored.

A rematch between the Brown Bomber from Detroit and the White Hope from Munich was scheduled for the summer of 1938. Caucasian expectations in Baltimore soared. It was Armageddon, the powers of darkness against the power of light.

In his Pulitzer Prize–winning autobiography *Growing Up*, Russell Baker writes:

> At last the night of the titanic battle finally arrived and I settled by my radio to attend upon the pivotal point of the modern age...
>
> At the bell Louis left his corner, appraised Schmeling the way a butcher eyes a side of beef, then punched him senseless in two minutes and nine seconds. Paralyzing in its brutal suddenness, it was the ultimate anticlimax for the white race.
>
> From Lemmon Street I heard the customary whooping and cheering. I went to the kitchen window...
>
> People were streaming out into the alley, pounding each other delightedly on the back and roaring with exultation. Then I saw someone start to move up the alley, out toward white territory, and the rest of the group, seized by an instinct to defy destiny, falling in behind him and moving en masse...
>
> There they were, marching right out into the middle of Lombard Street as though it was their own street...
>
> Joe Louis had given them the courage to assert their right to use a public thoroughfare, and there wasn't a white person down there to dispute it. It was the first civil rights demonstration I ever saw and it was completely spontaneous, ignited by the finality with which Joe Louis had destroyed the theory of white supremacy. The march lasted maybe five minutes, only as long as it took the entire throng to move slowly down the full

length of the block. Then they turned the corner and went back into the alleys and, I guess, felt better than most of them had felt for a long time.[2]

Does this sound like the victorious life in Christ? No! It was one of the many faces of the victorious limp.

Fifty years after Louis's first-round knockout, there are parts of America where to be black is not beautiful but bastard. Tonight, one in five people in the U.S. will go to bed hungry. Thirty million more are undernourished. Many are committed Christians. Is this the victorious life?

When our social system condemned blacks to the back of the bus, forced them to study in shacks and work in toilets, forbade them our sidewalks and our pews, barred them from hotels and restaurants, from movie theaters and restrooms, was this the victorious life?

Most of the descriptions of the victorious life do not match the reality of my own. Hyperbole, bloated rhetoric, and grandiose testimonies create the impression that once Jesus is acknowledged as Lord, the Christian life becomes a picnic on a green lawn—marriage blossoms into connubial bliss, physical health flourishes, acne disappears, and sinking careers suddenly soar. The victorious life is proclaimed to mean that everybody is a winner. An attractive twenty-year-old accepts Jesus and becomes Miss America; a floundering lawyer conquers alcoholism and whips F. Lee Bailey in court; a tenth-round draft choice for the Green Bay Packers goes to the Pro Bowl. Miracles occur, conversions abound, church attendance skyrockets, ruptured relationships get healed, shy people become gregarious, and the Atlanta Braves win the World Series. Idyllic descriptions of victory in Jesus are more often colored by cultural and personal expectations than by Christ and the ragamuffin gospel.

The New Testament depicts another picture of the victorious life: Jesus on Calvary. The biblical image of the victorious life reads more like the victorious limp. Jesus was victorious not because He never flinched, talked back, or questioned; but having flinched, talked back, and questioned, He remained faithful.

What makes authentic disciples is not visions, ecstasies, biblical mastery of chapter and verse, or spectacular success in the ministry, but a capacity for faithfulness. Buffeted by the fickle winds of failure, battered by their own unruly emotions, and bruised by rejection and ridicule, authentic disciples may have stumbled and frequently fallen, endured lapses and relapses, gotten handcuffed to the fleshpots, and wandered into a far country. Yet they kept coming back to Jesus.

After life has lined their faces a little, many followers of Jesus come into a coherent sense of themselves for the first time. When they modestly claim, "I am still a ragamuffin, but I'm different," they are right. Where sin abounded, grace has more abounded.

The portrait of Peter, the rock who proved to be a sand-pile, speaks to every ragamuffin across the generations. Lloyd Ogilvie notes:

Peter had built his whole relationship with Jesus Christ on his assumed capacity to be adequate. That's why he took his denial of the Lord so hard. His strength, loyalty, and faithfulness were his self-generated assets of discipleship. The fallacy in Peter's mind was this: He believed his relationship was dependent on his consistency in producing the qualities he thought had earned him the Lord's approval.

Many of us face the same problem. We project into the Lord our own measured standard of acceptance. Our whole understanding of him is based in a *quid pro quo* of bartered love. He will love us if we are good, moral, and diligent. But we have turned the tables; we try to live so that he will love us, rather than living because he has already loved us.[3]

During the supper of His love, Jesus turned and said to Peter, "I tell you solemnly, this very night, before the cock crows, you will have disowned me three times." Remember Peter's hollow boast? "Even if I have to die with you, I will never disown you." Brimming with confidence, Peter relied on his own resources. But today these words are a song of praise to Peter. His restoration to grace proved to be such a re-creation that his protest is no longer an empty boast but a prophecy of God's unyielding truth. For Peter will die rather than betray his Master, and he will forever remember his unfaithfulness as the moment of the triumph of grace and Christ's conquering love.

A story: Virtuoso violinist Pinchas Zukerman was giving a master class to a group of young artists who had come from the four corners of the world to the Aspen Music Festival. The auditorium was filled with their peers and distinguished teachers and performers; the atmosphere was electric. To each of the talented performers Zukerman offered friendly advice and encouragement, discussing their playing in detail and invariably picking up his own violin to demonstrate finer points of technique and interpretation.

Finally came the turn of a young musician who performed brilliantly. When the applause subsided, Zukerman complimented the artist, then walked over to his own violin, caressed it, tucked it under his chin, paused a long moment, and then, without playing a note or uttering a word, gently placed it back in its case. Once more the applause broke out and this time it was deafening, in recognition of the master who could pay so gracious a compliment.[4]

After his triple denial, what future would have awaited Peter if he had had to depend on my patience, understanding, and compassion? Instead of a shrug, sneer, slap, or curse, Jesus responded with the subtlest and most gracious compliment imaginable. He named Peter the leader of the faith community and entrusted him with authority to preach the Good News in the power of the Spirit.

The limping Peter's betrayal of the Master, like so many of our own moral relapses and refusals of grace, was not a terminal failure but the occasion for painful personal growth in fidelity. It is not unrealistic to presume that later, Peter praised God for the servant girl in Caiaphas's courtyard who turned him into a sniveling coward. In this context, small wonder that Augustine would paraphrase the words of Paul: "That for those who love God everything works unto good, even sin."

At some point in each of our lives, we were deeply touched

by a profound encounter with Jesus Christ. It was a mountaintop experience, a moment of immense consolation. We were
swept up in peace, joy, certitude, love. Quite simply, we were
overcome. Our minds and hearts resonated with awe and wonder. We were deeply moved for a few hours, days, or weeks, and
eventually returned to the routine occupations of our daily existence. We did not get unraveled.

Slowly we got caught up in the demands of ministry or
career and the distractions our busy world offers. We began to
treat Jesus like the old friend from Brooklyn whom we dearly
loved in years past but have gradually lost track of. Of course, it
was unintentional. We simply allowed circumstances to drive us
apart. On a recent visit to that city it never crossed our mind to
contact Him. We had become preoccupied with something
else, even though it was far less life-giving and captivating. It is
possible we may never love anyone as much as we loved him,
but even the memory has grown dim.

Heightened by the agnosticism of inattention—the lack
of personal discipline over media bombardment, mind control, sterile conversation, private prayer, and the subjugation
of the senses—the presence of Jesus grows more and more
remote. Just as the failure to be attentive dissolves confidence
and communion in a human relationship, so inattention to
the Holy unravels the fabric of the divine relationship.
"Thorns and thistles choke the unused path." A verdant heart
becomes a devastated vineyard. As we periodically close off God
to our consciousness by looking the other way, our hearts are
chilled. Christian agnostics don't deny a personal God; they
display their unbelief by ignoring the sacred. The paltriness of

our lives is mute testimony to the shabby furniture of our souls. And so our days become more and more trivial.

We get caught in a hectic maze. Rising when the clock determines. Battered by news headlines that seem remote and beyond our reach. Jangled by all the mechanical operations that launch us into activity and productivity. Tested by traffic, forced to calculate time and distance to the second. Elevators and phones and gadgets guide us through necessary interactions and keep human interactions superficial and at a minimum. Our concentration is interspersed by meetings and small crises. At the end of the day we rewind ourselves: traffic, automation, headlines, until we set that alarm clock to dictate tomorrow's awakening. Routines of ticking and timing. Little room for responding humanly and humanely to the day's events; little time to enter into the wisdom and freshness and the promise of its opportunities. We feel our lives closing in, confining, and conforming us.[5]

We settle in and settle down to lives of comfortable piety and well-fed virtue. We grow complacent and lead practical lives. Our feeble attempts at prayer are filled with stilted phrases addressed to an impassive deity. Even times of worship become trivialized.

This is the victorious limp often lived by this writer. At different times on the journey I have tried to fill the emptiness that frequently comes with God's presence through a variety of substitutes—writing, preaching, traveling, television, movies, ice cream, shallow relationships, sports, music, daydreaming, alcohol, etc. As Annie Dillard says, "There is always an enormous temptation to diddle around making itsy-bitsy friends and meals and journeys for itsy-bitsy years on end."[6] Along the way I opted for slavery and lost the desire for freedom. I loved my captivity and imprisoned myself in the desire for things I hated. I hardened my heart against true love. I abandoned prayer and took flight from the simple sacredness of my life. On some given day when grace overtook me and I returned to prayer, I half-expected Jesus to ask, "Who dat?"

None of my failures in faithfulness have proved terminal. Again and again radical grace has gripped me in the depths of my being, brought me to accept ownership of my infidelities, and led me back to the fifth step of the AA program: "Acknowledge to God, another human being, and myself the exact nature of my wrongdoing."

The forgiveness of God is gratuitous liberation from guilt. Paradoxically, the conviction of personal sinfulness becomes the occasion of encounter with the merciful love of the redeeming God. "There will be more rejoicing in heaven over one sinner repenting…" (Luke 15:7). In his brokenness, the repentant prodigal knew an intimacy with his father that his sinless, self-righteous brother would never know.

When Jesus forgave the sins of the paralytic, some scribes thought to themselves, "Who but God can forgive sins?" (Mark 2:7). How enlightened they were in their blindness! Only God knows how to pardon. Our clumsy human attempts at forgiveness often create more problems than they solve. In condescending fashion we crush and humiliate the sinner with our unbearable largesse. He may feel forgiven but utterly bereft of reassurance, consolation, and encouragement. Only God knows how to pardon and put all four together. The prodigal's father said, in effect, "Hush, child. I don't need to know where you've been or what you've been up to."

The gospel of grace announces, *Forgiveness precedes repentance.* The sinner is accepted before he pleads for mercy. He need only receive God's gift. Total amnesty. Gratuitous pardon.

> God alone can make forgiveness something glorious to remember. He's so glad to absolve us that those who've afforded him that joy feel, not like disagreeable, trouble-some pests, but like pampered children, understood and heartened, pleasing and useful to him, and infinitely better than they thought. "O happy fault!" they could cry. If we weren't sinners and didn't need pardon more than bread, we'd have no way of knowing how deep God's love is.[7]

When the prodigal son limped home from his lengthy binge of waste and wandering, boozing and womanizing, his motives were mixed at best. He said to himself, "How many of my father's hired men have all the food they want and more, and here am I dying of hunger! I will leave this place and go to my father" (Luke 15:17–18). The ragamuffin stomach was not churning with compunction because he had broken his father's heart. He stumbled home simply to survive. His sojourn in a far country had left him bankrupt. The days of wine and roses had left him dazed and disillusioned. The wine soured and the roses withered. His declaration of independence had reaped an unexpected harvest: not freedom, joy, and new life but bondage, gloom, and a brush with death. His fair-weather friends had shifted their allegiance when his piggy bank emptied. Disenchanted with life, the wastrel weaved his way home, not from a burning desire to see his father, but just to stay alive.

For me, the most touching verse in the entire Bible is the father's response: "While he was still a long way off, his father saw him and was moved with pity. He ran to the boy, clasped him in his arms and kissed him" (Luke 15:20). I am moved that the father didn't cross-examine the boy, bully him, lecture him on ingratitude, or insist on any high motivation. He was so overjoyed at the sight of his son that he ignored all the canons of prudence and parental discretion and simply welcomed him home. The father took him back just as he was.

What a word of encouragement, consolation, and comfort! We don't have to sift our hearts and analyze our intentions before returning home. Abba just wants us to show up. We don't have to tarry at the tavern until purity of heart arrives. We don't have to be shredded with sorrow or crushed with contrition. We don't have to be perfect or even very good before God will accept us. We don't have to wallow in guilt, shame, remorse, and self-condemnation. Even if we still nurse a secret nostalgia for the far country, Abba falls on our neck and kisses us.

Even if we come back because we couldn't make it on our own, God will welcome us. He will seek no explanations about our sudden appearance. He is glad we are there and wants to give us all we desire.

Henri Nouwen writes:

> In my mind's eye, I see Rembrandt's painting *The Return of the Prodigal Son*. The dim-eyed old father holds his returned son close to his chest with an unconditional love. Both of his hands, one strong and masculine, the other gentle and feminine, rest on his son's shoulders. He does not look at his son but feels his young, tired body and lets him rest in his embrace. His immense red cape is like the wings of a mother bird covering her fragile nestling. He seems to think only one thing: He is back home, and I am so glad to have him with me again.
>
> So why delay? God is standing there with open arms, waiting to embrace me. He won't ask any questions about my past. Just having me back is all he desires.[8]

The parable of the prodigal is one of the many faces of faithfulness. It is also an earthy and honest portrait of the victorious limp.

So is the Academy Award winner for best film of 1966, *A Man for All Seasons,* the gripping narrative of one man's faithfulness to himself and to Christ at all costs. Thomas More, the chancellor of England, has been imprisoned in the Tower of London for his refusal to obey the Crown. He is visited by his daughter Meg, who pleads with him to change his mind and save his life. More explains that if he took the oath of allegiance to King Henry VIII, he would compromise his conscience and betray Jesus. She argues that it is not his fault that the state is three-quarters bad and, if he chooses to suffer for it, he is making himself a hero. Her father replies:

> Meg, if we lived in a state where virtue was profitable, common sense would make us good, and greed would make us saintly. And we'd live animals or angels in the happy land that needs no heroes. But since in fact we see that avarice, anger, envy, pride, sloth, lust, and stupidity commonly profit far beyond humility, chastity, fortitude, justice, and thought, and have to choose to be human at all, why then perhaps we must stand fast a little, even at the risk of being heroes.[9]

In 1535, More went to the scaffold cheerfully in the royal freedom of a Christian man. He prayed briefly for God's mercy, embraced the executioner—who begged his forgiveness—confessed his Christian faith, and called on all present to pray for the King, saying that he died "the King's good servant, but God's first." His last words were a joke about his beard, which he arranged on the block so that it should not be cut, since his beard, at least, had committed no treason.

Thomas More, a man of the world in secular dress living in a secular city and surrounded by family, possessions, and the duties of public life, was *faithful*. Not because he was without faults and sins; he had them, like every one of us, and confessed them often before his death. But with all his weaknesses and flaws he made a radical choice to be true to himself and his Christ in the supreme test of martyrdom.

In 1929, G. K. Chesterton predicted, "Sir Thomas More is more important at this moment than at any moment since his death, even perhaps the great moment of dying; but he is not quite so important as he will be in a hundred years' time."[10] His life is a timeless statement—it is possible to live in this world soberly, honestly, unfanatically, unpietistically, seriously, and at the same time, joyfully: faithful. What is the message of this man's life? Make a radical choice in faith, despite all your sinfulness, and sustain it through ordinary daily life for Christ the Lord and His kingdom.

The mature Christians I have met along the way are those who have failed and have learned to live gracefully with their failure. Faithfulness requires the courage to risk everything on Jesus, the willingness to keep growing, and the readiness to risk failure throughout our lives. What do these things mean, specifically?

Risking everything on Jesus: The ragamuffin gospel says we can't lose, because we have nothing to lose. Faithfulness to Jesus implies that with all our sins, scars, and insecurities, we stand with Him; that we are formed and informed by His Word; that we acknowledge that abortion and nuclear weapons are two sides of the same hot coin minted in hell; that we stand upright beside the Prince of Peace and refuse to bow before the shrine of national security; that we are a life-giving and not a death-dealing people of God; that we live under the sign of the cross and not the sign of the bomb.

The willingness to keep growing: Unfaithfulness is a refusal to become, a rejection of grace (grace that is inactive is an illusion), and the refusal to be oneself. Long ago I read a prayer composed by the late Gen. Douglas MacArthur:

> Youth is not a period of time. It is a state of mind, a
> result of the will, a quality of the imagination, a victory
> of courage over timidity, of the taste for adventure over
> the love of comfort. A man doesn't grow old because
> he has lived a certain number of years. A man grows
> old when he deserts his ideal. The years may wrinkle
> his skin, but deserting his ideal wrinkles his soul.
> Preoccupations, fears, doubts, and despair are the ene-
> mies which slowly bow us toward earth and turn us
> into dust before death. You will remain young as long
> as you are open to what is beautiful, good, and great;
> receptive to the messages of other men and women, of
> nature, and of God. If one day you should become bit-
> ter, pessimistic, and gnawed by despair, may God have
> mercy on your old man's soul.

The readiness to risk failure: Many of us are haunted by our
failure to have done with our lives what we longed to accomplish. The disparity between our ideal self and our real self, the
grim specter of past infidelities, the awareness that I am not living what I believe, the relentless pressure of conformity, and the
nostalgia for lost innocence reinforces a nagging sense of existential guilt: *I have failed.* This is the cross we never expected,
and the one we find hardest to bear.

One morning at prayer, I heard this word: *Little brother, I
witnessed a Peter who claimed that he did not know Me, a James
who wanted power in return for service to the kingdom, a Philip*

who failed to see the Father in Me, and scores of disciples who were convinced I was finished on Calvary. The New Testament has many examples of men and women who started out well and then faltered along the way. Yet on Easter night I appeared to Peter. James is not remembered for his ambition but for the sacrifice of his life for Me. Philip did see the Father in Me when I pointed the way, and the disciples who despaired had enough courage to recognize Me when we broke bread at the end of the road to Emmaus. My point, little brother, is this: I expect more failure from you than you expect from yourself.

The ragamuffin who sees his life as a voyage of discovery and runs the risk of failure has a better feel for faithfulness than the timid man who hides behind the law and never finds out who he is at all. Winston Churchill said it well: "Success is never final; failure is never fatal. It is courage that counts."

One night a dear friend of Roslyn's named Joe McGill was praying over this passage in John: "In the beginning was the Word: the Word was with God and the Word was God. The Word became flesh, he lived among us" (John 1:1, 14). In the bright darkness of faith, he heard Jesus say, *Yes, the Word was made flesh. I chose to enter your broken world and limp through life with you.*

On the last day, when we arrive at the Great Cabin in the Sky, many of us will be bloodied, battered, bruised, and limping. But by God and by Christ, there will be a light in the window and a "Welcome Home" sign on the door.

Chapter Eleven

A Touch of Folly

*I*n 1982, when I moved from Clearwater, Florida, to New Orleans, I did some homework on the origins of the Christian faith in the area. In sifting through the archives, I came across a fascinating piece of information.

Over a hundred years ago in the Deep South, a phrase so common in our Christian culture today, *born again,* was seldom or never used. Rather, the phrase used to describe the breakthrough into a personal relationship with Jesus Christ was "I was seized by the power of a great affection." These words described both the initiative of God and the explosion within the heart when Jesus, instead of being a face on a holy card with long hair and a robe with many folds, became real, alive, and Lord of one's personal and professional life. *Seized by the power of a great affection* was a visceral description of the phenomenon

of Pentecost, authentic conversion, and the release of the Holy
Spirit. The phrase lent new meaning to the old Russian proverb,
"Those who have the disease called Jesus will never be cured."

In March 1986, I was privileged to spend an afternoon with
an Amish family in Lancaster, Pennsylvania. I have long cherished a deep respect and admiration for the Amish community.
We each have a dream, a vision of life that corresponds to our
convictions, embodies our uniqueness, and expresses what is
life-giving within us. Whether altruistic or ignoble, the dream
gives definition to our lives, influences the decisions we make,
the steps we take, and the words we speak. Daily we make
choices that are either consistent with or contrary to our vision.
A life of integrity is born of fidelity to the dream. As a community the Amish, at great personal cost, have carved out a lifestyle
that gives flesh and bones to their dream.

Jonas Zook is an eighty-two-year-old widower. He and
his children raise piglets for their livelihood. The oldest,
Barbara, fifty-seven, manages the household. The three younger
children—Rachel, fifty-three; Elam, forty-seven; and Sam,
forty-five—are all severely retarded. When I arrived at noon
with two friends, little Elam—about four feet tall, heavy-set,
thickly bearded, and wearing the black Amish outfit with the
circular hat—was coming out of the barn some fifty yards
away, pitchfork in hand. He had never laid eyes on me in his
life; yet, when he saw me step out of the car, this little mon-
goloid dropped the pitchfork and ran lickety-split in my
direction. From two feet away he flung himself at me, wrapped
his arms around my neck, his legs around my waist, and kissed
me on the lips with fierce intensity for a full thirty seconds.

Well, I was temporarily stunned and terribly self-conscious. But in the twinkle of an eye, Jesus set me free from propriety. I buried my lips into Elam's and returned his kiss with the same enthusiasm. Then he jumped down, wrapped both his hands around my right arm, and led me on a tour of the farm.

A half hour later, Elam sat next to me at lunch. Midway through the meal I turned around to say something. Inadvertently, my right elbow slammed into Elam's rib cage. He didn't wince, he didn't groan; he wept like a two-year-old child. His next move undid me.

Elam came over to my chair, planted himself on my lap, and kissed me even harder on the lips. Then he kissed my eyes, nose, forehead, and cheeks.

And there was Brennan, dazed, dumbstruck, weeping, and suddenly *seized by the power of a great affection.* In his utter simplicity little Elam Zook was an icon of Jesus Christ. Why? Because at that moment his love for me did not stem from any attractiveness or lovability of mine. It was not conditioned by any response on my part. Elam loved me whether I was kind or unkind, pleasant or nasty. His love arose from a source outside of himself and myself.

As often happens in a profound moment like that, I will recall a line from a book I had read years earlier. Discussing the tragic history of Native Americans, the author noted that the Iroquois attributed divinity to retarded children, gave them an honored place in the tribe, and treated them as gods. In their unself-conscious freedom they were a transparent window into the Great Spirit—into the heart of Jesus Christ who loves us as we are and not as we should be, in the state of grace or disgrace, beyond caution, boundary, regret, or breaking point.[1]

In a world that is torn and tearing, it takes a touch of folly to believe that "even when our choices are destructive and their consequences hurtful, God's love remains unwavering. Thus, regardless of our own insulation and defensiveness, God is constantly open and vulnerable to us."[2] As the sea of suffering humanity swells, we are hard-pressed for proofs that the crucified risen Jesus has prevailed over every principality, power, and dominion, discarded them like a garment, and led them captive in His victory procession.

The sad plight of Native Americans is a haunting memory that refuses to go away. They are homeless, having lost their culture, their land, their pride, and their hope. Refugees from Afghanistan, Haiti, Cuba, and the South Pacific Islands stream to our shores and are often deposited in slums and barrios unfit for human habitation. Bag ladies, derelicts, and the mentally disturbed stalk the street of our cities. Small farmers are wiped out by the encroachment of agribusiness. Strip-mining has raped the land. White-collar crime on Wall Street and governmental fraud in Washington devastate American morale. AIDS victims are ostracized and shunned as undesirables. The drug epidemic ravages our youth and puts all our tomorrows up for grabs. Venal clergymen are a dime a dozen. Anti-Semitism and racism are scars on the national conscience.

After two thousand years the Body of Christ is still dreadfully divided by doctrine, history, and day-to-day living. Scabrous stories about Christian disunity pepper the pages of periodicals and newspapers. The Body of Truth is bleeding from a thousand wounds. Small wonder that many Christians today are bedraggled, beat-up, and burnt-out. The bleak landscape of the global village has introduced discouragement, disillusionment, and what Parker Palmer calls "functional atheism"—the belief that nothing is happening unless we are making it happen. Though our Christian language pays lip service to God, our way of functioning assumes that God is dead or in a coma. Being seized by the power of a great affection does not seem to relate to the real world in which we live. Does it not require a fair measure of lunacy to listen to the loony tunes of the ragamuffin gospel?

Yes it does! As Zorba the Greek said to his employer, "It's difficult, boss, very difficult. You need a touch of folly to do it; folly, d'you see? You have to risk everything!"[3] In the final analysis, discipleship is a life of sublime madness.

The truth of the gospel of Jesus Christ does not rise and fall on the issues of corrupt clergy, the exploitation of the poor, the stinginess of multinationals, or the irrational fanaticism of modern dictatorships. It deserves to be accepted or rejected for what it is: an answer to the most fundamental questions a person may ask: Is life absurd or does it have a purpose? Jesus replies that not only do our lives have purpose but God has directly intervened in human affairs to make abundantly clear what that purpose is. What is the nature of Ultimate Reality? Jesus responds that the Really Real is generous, forgiving, saving love. In the end, will life triumph over death? With unshaken confidence Jesus answers, *The kingdom of My Father cannot be overcome, even by death. In the end everything will be all right. Nothing can harm you permanently; no loss is lasting, no defeat more than transitory, no disappointment is conclusive.*

Suffering, failure, loneliness, sorrow, discouragement, and death will be part of your journey, but the kingdom of God will conquer all these horrors. No evil can resist grace forever.

If you reject the ragamuffin gospel and turn your back on Christianity, do so because you find the answers of Jesus incredible, blasphemous, or hopelessly hopeful.

> Reject Christianity, if you will, out of motives of cynicism; turn away from it because you believe. Reality is malign and punitive; choose a God that is cantankerous, vindictive, or forgetful, or determined to keep man in his place, if such a God is more to your choosing. If you cannot accept the idea that love is at the core of the universe, that is your privilege. If you do not believe that the Absolute passionately wants to be our friend and our lover, then by all means reject such a seemingly absurd notion. If you do not believe that we have the enthusiasm and the strength and the courage and the creativity to love one another as friends, then quickly cast aside such an incredible idea into the trash can. And if you think it is ridiculous to believe that life will triumph over death, then don't bother with Christianity, because you can't be a Christian unless you believe that.[4]

In first-century Palestine, the people of Judea and Galilee fudged and hedged on the proclamation of the reign of God. Jesus announced that the old era was done, that a new age had dawned, and the only appropriate response was to be captivated with joy and wonder.

His listeners did not say, "Yes, Rabbi, we believe You," or "No, Rabbi, we think You are a fool." Rather, they said, "What about the sap-suckin' Romans?" or "When are You going to produce an apocalyptic sign?" or "Why aren't You and Your disciples within the Jewish Law?" or "Whose side do You take in the various legal controversies?"

Jesus replied that the Romans were not the issue, the Law was not the issue, and cosmic miracles were not the issue. The relentless love of God was the issue, and in the face of that revelation, the Romans and the Torah were secondary. But His audience stubbornly refused to concede that the Torah could possibly be secondary or that the Roman domination of Palestine could be marginal. The Torah and Rome—these were the relevant issues, the gut problems. "What do You have to say about *them*, Rabbi?"

Once again Jesus responded that He did not come to discuss the Law nor to challenge the Roman Empire. He had come to herald the Good News that the Really Real is love and to invite men and women to a joyous response to that love.

Sober, hard-headed, realistic critics simply shook their heads. "Why doesn't He address the critical questions?"

Since the day that Jesus first appeared on the scene, we have developed vast theological systems, organized world-wide churches, filled libraries with brilliant Christological scholarship, engaged in earthshaking controversies, and embarked on crusades, reforms, and renewals. Yet there are still precious few of us with sufficient folly to make the mad exchange of everything for Christ; only a remnant with the confidence to risk everything on the gospel of grace; only a minority who stagger about with the delirious joy of the man who found the buried treasure.

It was cynicism, pessimism, and despair that shadowed the ministry of Jesus and, as the old French proverb goes, *"Plus ça change, plus c'est la même chose"*—the more things change, the more they stay the same.

At the risk of sounding like a country cracker cowboy preacher, allow me to raise some intimate, personal questions about your relationship with Jesus of Nazareth. Do you live each day in the blessed assurance that you have been saved by the unique grace of our Lord Jesus Christ? After falling flat on your face, are you still firmly convinced that the fundamental structure of reality is not works but grace? Are you moody and melancholy because you are still striving for the perfection that comes from your own efforts and not from faith in Jesus Christ? Are you shocked and horrified when you fail? Are you really aware that you don't have to change, grow, or be good to be loved?

Are you as certain of the triumph of good over evil as the fermentation of dough by yeast? Though on a given day you may be more depressed than anything else, is the general orientation of your life toward peace and joy? Are you diminished by other people's perception of you or your own definition of yourself? Do you possess that touch of folly to transcend doubt, fear, and self-hatred and accept that you are accepted?

If not, you probably belong to the brotherhood of the bedraggled, beat-up, and burnt-out. You may feel like a charred log in a fireplace, totally drained of energy, and unable to light a fire in yourself. Your personal inner resources appear to be exhausted. Louis Savary describes the brotherhood this way:

> Their life is full of demands from others. They seem to be living at least three lives; everyone wants a piece of them; they can't say no, yet they have no time to do what they have already said yes to…. They cannot seem to find the necessary clarity and information on which to base decisions…they make a great investment in relationships and get little gratitude, feedback, or even acknowledgment from others. "Although nonreciprocity is inevitable and acceptable," writes Mitchell, "it is also draining. No one can function long in a helping profession without feeling its impact."[5]

The first step toward rejuvenation begins with accepting where you are and exposing your poverty, frailty, and emptiness to the love that is everything. Don't try to feel anything, think anything, or do anything. With all the goodwill in the world you cannot make anything happen. Don't force prayer. Simply relax in the presence of the God you half believe in and ask for a touch of folly.

The Indian poet Tagore puts it this way:

> No, it is not yours to open buds into blossoms.
> Shake the bud, strike it; it is beyond your power to
>   make it blossom.
> Your touch soils it, you tear its petals to pieces and
>   strew them in the dust.

But no colours appear, and no perfume.
Ah! It is not for you to open the bud into blossom.

He who can open the bud does it so simply.
He gives it a glance, and the life-sap stirs through
    its veins.
At his breath the flower spreads its wings and flutters
    in the wind.
Colours flush out like heart-longings, the perfume
    betrays a sweet secret.
He who can open the bud does it so simply.[6]

Next, try this simple exercise in faith: Gently close your eyes and assume any position that is comfortable so long as you keep your spine straight—standing, sitting, kneeling or lying on your back with your knees bent. Imagine Jesus glancing at you either the way He glanced at the apostle John in the Upper Room when, in an incredible gesture of intimacy, he laid his head on Jesus' chest; or the way He looked at the sinful woman washing His feet with her tears and drying them with her hair. For ten minutes pray over and over the first strophe of Psalm 23: "Yahweh is my shepherd, I lack nothing."

For the next ten minutes pray over this passage from Hosea and wherever you see the word *Israel,* replace it with your own name:

When Israel was a child I loved him,
    out of Egypt I called my son.
Yet it was I who taught Ephraim to walk,

who took them in my arms;
I drew them with human cords,
  with bands of love;
I fostered them like one
  who raises an infant to his cheeks;
Yet, though I stooped to feed my child,
  they did not know that I was their healer.
How could I give you up, O Ephraim,
  or deliver you up, O Israel?
How could I treat you as Admah,
  or make you like Zeboiim?
My heart is overwhelmed,
  my pity is stirred.
I will not give vent to my blazing anger,
  I will not destroy Ephraim again;
For I am God and not man,
  the Holy One present among you;
I will not let the flames consume you.
(Hosea 11:1, 3–4, 8–9, NAB)

Finally, for the last five minutes of this faith exercise read aloud slowly these three texts:

But look, I am going to seduce her and lead her into the desert and speak to her heart. There I shall give her back her vineyards, and make the Vale of Achor a gateway of hope. There she will respond as when she was young, as on the day when she came up from Egypt. (Hosea 2:14–15)

Yahweh called me when I was in the womb, before my
birth he had pronounced my name... Can a woman
forget her baby at the breast, feel no pity for the child
she has borne? Even if these were to forget, I shall not
forget you. Look, I have engraved you on the palms of
my hands, your ramparts are ever before me. (Isaiah
49:1, 15–16)

After saying this, what can we add? If God is for us, who
can be against us? Since he did not spare his own Son,
but gave him up for the sake of all of us, then can we
not expect that with him he will freely give us all his
gifts? (Romans 8:31–32)

Should you ever have the opportunity to celebrate Easter
in France, whether it be a large metropolis such as Paris,
Bordeaux, or Lyon or a small village such as Saint-Remy
(where I lived for six months), you will see one phrase written
on the walls of buildings or the sides of buses in script or black
print. You will hear the one phrase sung, chanted, and recited
in the churches. You will hear it exchanged as an Easter greeting as people pass on the street: *"L'amour de Dieu est folie!"*—The
love of God is folly.

In these pages I have stuttered and stammered in a halting
attempt to hint at the shattering reality of the furious love of
God. Like an old miner panning the stream of his memories, I
have reached back into the Scriptures to listen to God's self-
disclosure. I have read hundreds of biblical, theological, and
spiritual books seeking deeper understanding of the gospel of

grace. I have freely employed story, imagery, poetry, symbolism, the language of metaphor, and prose narrative to communicate something of the passionate love of our passionate God. Acknowledging my own limitations, I am not going to be hard on myself because I know there is going to come a time and there is going to be a place where we can say it all. The secret of the mystery is, God is always greater. No matter how great we think Him to be, His love is always greater.

The story goes that Thomas Aquinas, perhaps the world's greatest theologian, toward the end of his life suddenly stopped writing. When his secretary complained that his work was unfinished, Thomas replied, "Brother Reginald, when I was at prayer a few months ago, I experienced something of the reality of Jesus Christ. That day, I lost all appetite for writing. In fact, all I have ever written about Christ seems now to me to be like straw."[7]

L'amour de Dieu est folie! It reaches out to ragamuffins everywhere. My only exhortation: Let us walk together. My only prayer: May Jesus Christ convert us to the folly of the gospel.

A Word After

Upon finishing this book, a thoughtful reader might ruminate, *Hmmm. He made a few good points, but the book seems one-sided. Brennan goes on and on about Abba, Jesus, radical grace, compassion, and the furious love of God, but says little about morality. I think he stacked the deck.*

The Bible is the love story of God with His people. God calls, pursues, forgives, and heals. Our response to His love is itself His gift.

Let us suppose you advanced me $1 million for my personal needs. A year later, you request that I begin making monthly interest-free payments of $10,000 on the debt. On the first day of each month I sit down to write the check just as the morning mail arrives. In the mail I find that you have sent me a $10,000 check to cover my payment. You continue this practice every month until the full amount of my debt is relieved. I am bewildered and protest, "But this is totally lopsided!"

God is enamored with His people and so intent upon a

response that He even provides the grace to respond. "May he enlighten the eyes of your mind so that you can see what hope his call holds for you, how rich is the glory of the heritage he offers among his holy people, and how extraordinarily great is the power that he has exercised for us believers; this accords with the strength of his power" (Ephesians 1:18–19).

The love of God is simply unimaginable. "So that Christ may live in your hearts through faith, and then, planted in love and built on love, with all God's holy people you will have the strength to grasp the breadth and the length, the height and the depth; so that, knowing the love of Christ, which is beyond knowledge, you may be filled with the utter fullness of God" (Ephesians 3:17–19).

Do we really hear what Paul is saying? Stretch, man, stretch! Let go of impoverished, circumscribed, and finite perceptions of God. The love of Christ is beyond all knowledge, beyond anything we can intellectualize or imagine. It is not a mild benevolence but a consuming fire. Jesus is so unbearably forgiving, so infinitely patient, and so unendingly loving that He provides us with the resources we need to live lives of gracious response. "Glory be to him whose power, working in us, can do infinitely more than we can ask or imagine" (Ephesians 3:20).

Does it sound like an easy religion?

Love has its own exigencies. It weighs and counts nothing but expects everything. Perhaps that explains our reluctance to risk. We know only too well that the gospel of grace is an irresistible call to love the same way. No wonder so many of us elect to surrender our souls to rules rather than to living in union with Love.

No greater sinners exist than those so-called Christians who disfigure the face of God, mutilate the gospel of grace, and intimidate others through fear. They corrupt the essential nature of Christianity. In Eugene Peterson's forceful phrase, "They are telling lies about God, and let them be cursed."

The North American church is at a critical juncture. The gospel of grace is being confused and compromised by silence, seduction, and outright subversion. The vitality of faith is jeopardized. The lying slogans of the fixers who carry religion like a sword of judgment pile up with impunity.

Let ragamuffins everywhere gather as a confessing church to cry out in protest. Revoke the licenses of religious leaders who falsify the idea of God. Sentence them to three years in solitude with the Bible as their only companion.

Mary Magdalene stands as a witness par excellence to the ragamuffin gospel. On Good Friday she watched as the man she loved got blown away in the most brutal and dehumanizing fashion. The focus of her attention, however, was not on suffering but the suffering Christ "who loved me and gave himself for me" (Galatians 2:20). Never allow these words to be interpreted as allegory in the life of Magdalene. The love of Jesus was a burning and divine reality to her: She would have been buried in history as some unknown hooker save for the Christ encounter.

She has no understanding of God, church, religion, prayer, or ministry except in terms of the Sacred Man who loved her and delivered Himself up for her. The unique place that Magdalene occupies in the history of discipleship owes not to her mysterious love for Jesus but to the miraculous transformation that His love wrought in her life. She simply let herself be loved. "The central truth for which Mary's life has come to stand is that it is possible to be delivered through love from the lowest depths to the shining heights where God dwelleth."[1]

Where sin abounded, grace abounded all the more.

When Jesus asked Peter on the Tiberian seashore, "Simon, son of John, do you love Me?" He added nothing else; what He said was enough. *Do you love Me? Can you allow My love to touch you in your weakness, set you free, and empower you there?* Thereafter, the only power Peter had was Jesus' love for him. He told and retold the story of his own unfaithfulness and how Jesus touched him. When he proclaimed the gospel of grace, he preached from his weakness the power of God. That is what converted the Roman world and what will convert us, and the people around us, if they see that the love of Christ has touched us.

The confessing church of American ragamuffins needs to join Magdalene and Peter in witnessing that Christianity is not primarily a moral code but a grace-laden mystery; it is not essentially a philosophy of love but a love affair; it is not keeping rules with clenched fists but receiving a gift with open hands.

Several years ago, the renowned evangelical theologian Francis Schaeffer wrote, "True spirituality consists in living moment to moment by the grace of Jesus Christ." This book lays no claim to originality; it is simply a commentary on Schaeffer's statement. As C. S. Lewis was fond of saying, people need more to be reminded than to be instructed.

The Scandal of Grace

Fifteen Years Later

J have been denounced publicly and privately as a heretic, schismatic, universalist, and cockeyed optimist. A Roman Catholic scholar informed me that I had out-Luthered Luther. I have been charged with not believing in the existence of hell, judgment, and damnation. One report out of Indiana scolded me for a selective use of biblical texts. I have been labeled "unbalanced," "spiritually immature," and "intellectually unhinged." A newspaper article in California challenged my doctrinal purity and moral rectitude.

The gospel of grace continues to scandalize.

The legalists, puritans, prophets of doom, and moral crusaders are having a hissy fit over the Pauline teaching of justification by grace through faith. They take umbrage at the freedom of the children of God and dismiss it as licentiousness. They do not want Christianity to help us become whole but to feel wretched under its burden. They seek to intimidate us, make us afraid, file through their exclusive pathway of righteousness, and control rather than liberate our lives. Their perverted spirit of legalism would cripple the human spirit and send us sagging under great spools of rules and regulations. The thrilling quality of their dedication—zealotry is always impressive—obscures the fact that they accept the gospel in theory and deny it in practice.

These critical comments sound harsh, but they are actually quite tame compared to Jesus' words in Matthew 23, where He excoriates legalists for the systemic nit-picking that obscures the face of a compassionate God. *Frauds! Liars! Hypocrites! Whitewashed tombs! Snakes!*—this is the untamed fury of Jesus at corrupt religious practice. (Of course, I am too well defended against my own rationalizations to see that I may not be as different from the hypocrites as I would like to think.)

Over the past decade, however, what St. Augustine called the *sensus fidelium*—the sense of the faithful—has overwhelmingly affirmed the truth of *The Ragamuffin Gospel.* The Holy Spirit dwells within ordinary people going about their everyday tasks, and they offer to the Body of Christ trustworthy ideas about God's love for us. In every age the church is saved by ragamuffins with an unerring discernment of spirits. In the third century, when two hundred bishops embraced the heretical doctrine of Arius denying the divinity of Christ, it was the *sensus fidelium* who refused to follow, thereby preserving the faith community from disintegration.

Since its original 1990 publication, *The Ragamuffin Gospel* has spawned a small cottage industry. Its theme inspired at least a dozen songs. The late Rich Mullins formed the Ragamuffin Band. Several books, poems, and paintings, and even a few bookstores carry the ragamuffin tag. Someone sent me a little cardboard box with a baking mix inside for making breakfast Rag-a-Muffins.

Why does this metaphor continue to captivate after all these years? I believe that it speaks to the spiritual condition of most of us. Ragamuffins are the *anawim* of the Hebrew Scriptures—the poor in spirit who, aware of their inner poverty and emptiness, threw themselves without hesitation on the mercy of God. They compounded a sense of personal powerlessness with unfailing trust in the love of God. They were indeed the remnant, the true Israel to whom the messianic promises had been made.

The way of the ragamuffin is a considerably different view of the Christian life than that of traditional church culture. It is rooted in Jesus' statement, "The Son of man came not to be served but to serve" (Matthew 20:28). Ragamuffins don't sit down to be served; they kneel down to serve. When there is food on their plate, they don't whine about the mystery meat or the soggy veggies; nor do they whimper about the monotonous menu or the cracked plate. Glad for a full stomach, they give thanks for the smallest gift. They do not grow impatient and irritable with the dismal service in department stores, because they so often fail to be good servants themselves.

Ragamuffins do not complain about the feeble preaching and the lifeless worship of their local church. They are happy to have a place to go where they can mingle with other beggars at the door of God's mercy. "Beggars know how to open their hands," writes Sue Monk Kidd, "trusting that the crumb of grace will fall."[1] Humbly acknowledging that they are proletarian folks powerless to achieve their heart's desires without divine help, they are grateful for the smallest crumb that tumbles from the preacher's mouth.

Long prayers and big words do not suit ragamuffins. Their mouthpiece is the tax collector in the temple: "God, be merciful to me, a sinner" (Luke 18:13). The ragamuffin knows that she is the tax collector and that refusing to admit it would make her a Pharisee. Tax collectors, nobodies, vagabonds, tramps of Jesus—ragamuffins laugh at their own vanity for wanting to be noticed and for being unnoticeable.

Neither are ragamuffins interested in pretensions to self-sufficiency. They know that any declaration of independence from the kindness of others is sheer folly. A Cajun would never ask, "Would you like a ride over to the city?" Rather, he would urge, "Can I carry you across the river?" The automatic "no" of pharisaic hubris must yield to the spontaneous "yes" of the needy.

"Yes" is a big word in the ragamuffin vocabulary, especially in response to the command of Jesus, "Courage! It's me! Don't be afraid" (Mark 6:50), and to the words of the disciple Jesus loved: "In love there is no room for fear, but perfect love drives out fear, because fear implies punishment, and no one who is afraid has come to perfection in love" (1 John 4:18). A little ragamuffin named Amy Welborn gives voice to the ragtag band:

Love may drive out fear, but some of us have to take John's challenge from the other direction first. We have to stop being afraid to make room for love. We can tell another person of our love easily enough. But if we harbor fears at the back of our minds—"Does he really love me? How could he?" or "If I love her, will she really return that love, or will she eventually betray me?"—we are holding back. We're cautious, yes, and perhaps that is sometimes wise. After all, who wants to be hurt? But can love flourish if hemmed in by doubts and fears? No.

I think it's the same with our love for God. Loving faith—handing our lives over to God in complete trust—can't happen when we hold back something out of fear, either the fear of punishment or the fear that the whole thing is a sham.

"Lord Jesus, I put my fears aside today and open my heart to you in trust."[2]

The longing for freedom from fear leads the ragamuffin to raw honesty about his predicament: the utter inability to self-generate trust. So he hurls himself on God's mercy and approaches the throne of grace with confidence, because "he rescues the needy who calls to him, and the poor who has no one to help. He has pity on the weak and the needy, and saves the needy from death" (Psalm 72:12–13).

No longer shifting the heavy suitcase from one hand to the other, the bedraggled, beat-up and burnt-out are emboldened by the testimony of the beloved disciple: "Our fearlessness towards him consists in this, that if we ask anything in accordance with his will he hears us. And if we know that he listens to whatever we ask him, we know that we already possess whatever we have asked of him" (1 John 5:14–15). After giving thanks for a cup of steaming hot coffee and her breakfast Rag-a-Muffin, she rests securely in the promise of Jesus: "Everything you ask and pray for, believe that you have it already, and it will be yours" (Mark 11:24). This is a level of trust that borders on chutzpah!

Without fail, personal experience of the love of Jesus Christ initiates trust. Radical dependence and trusting surrender are the systole and diastole of the ragamuffin's palpitating heart. But although ragamuffins may be softhearted, they are hardheaded. They do not live in a dreamy, spaced-out state, pontificating about the victorious Christian life. They form the mendicant church, not the church triumphal. Acknowledging the reality of their own impoverished lives, they know they cannot survive without the divine dole for their daily bread. Their security rests in having no security.

Ragamuffins never despise their material and/or spiritual poverty, because they deem themselves wealthy beyond compare. They have found the treasure in the field (see Matthew 13:44). Nothing compares to the kingdom of God. In their eyes its worth is beyond all worth. Measurement fails. Scales tip over. All calculation collapses in this infinity. This is the ragamuffin's secret, which nominal Christians do not understand, but for which martyrs have given their lives. For the sake of the kingdom of God, thousands upon thousands have had their possessions confiscated, homelands seized, and families, careers, and good names sacrificed.

The nominal just don't get it. They hear the Word of God, but it does not speak to them interiorly. The unseen world does not exist. The love story of the Bible is nice for children in Sunday school but not for rational adults. Faith is a relic of the Middle Ages. You can't pay the rent, cook soup, or purchase a computer with religion. What matters is muscle, intelligence, connections, and stronger battalions. The rest is opium for the people. The nominal do not know the secret. The treasure is hidden from their eyes. The values and lifestyle of the ragamuffin rabble are simply incomprehensible.

It is the ragamuffin alone who rightly comprehends what life is really all about. No effort is too great, no venture too daring, no sacrifice too painful for the sake of the kingdom. Her greatest risk is still too small. And yet at prayer she often experiences the "null"—the felt absence of God. She does not insist on visions and locutions. Peak spiritual experiences are rare in her interior poverty. She is not greedy for comforts, spiritual consolations included. She lives in the Void but knows with Bede Griffiths that the Void is completely saturated with love.

Ragamuffins are simple, direct, and honest. Their speech is unaffected. They are slow to claim, "God told me…" As they make their way through the world, they bear wordless, prophetic witness.

Perhaps the supreme achievement of the Holy Spirit in the life of ragamuffins is the miraculous movement from self-rejection to self-acceptance. It is not based on therapy or the power of positive thinking; it is anchored in their personal experience of the acceptance of Jesus Christ. They are not saints, but they seek spiritual growth. They accept counsel and constructive criticism with ease. They stumble often, but they do not spend endless hours in self-recrimination. They quickly repent, offering the broken moment to the Lord. Their past has been crucified with Christ and no longer exists, except in the deep recesses of eternity.

Immersed in the sinful human condition, the ragamuffin struggles to be faithful to Jesus. Taking up the cross of his wounded self each day, he battles with fatigue, loneliness, failure, depression, rejection, and the sting of discovering untrustworthiness in the person he thought most trustworthy. The ragamuffin road always leads to Calvary.

Ragamuffins are haunted by Francis Thompson's words in his poem "The Hound of Heaven":

> Though I knew
> it was His love who followed,
> yet was I sore adread,
> lest having Him
> I must have naught beside.

Is Jesus enough? Is His love mediated through spouse, children, and friends enough? Must I grasp for something else? Will the incessant clanging of my addictions, wants, and desires steal my Promethean fire? Must I wander again into the far country in search of God knows what? I harbor one legitimate fear: Having been given a seat at the wedding feast, the thought of ever going back into the misery and filth—the cold and the darkness of the highways and hedges, the streets and the alleys of a self-centered life—fills me with holy dread. From the depth of my heart I pray, in the words of St. Augustine,

"Lord Jesus, don't let me lie when I say that I love you...and protect me, for today I could betray you."

The ragamuffin church is a place of promise and possibility, of adventure and discovery, a community of compassion on the move, strangers and exiles in a foreign land en route to the heavenly Jerusalem. Ragamuffins are a pilgrim people who have checked into the hotel of earth overnight, bags unpacked and ready to go. Regrouping and retrenching, squatting and debating, are not their poses and postures.

In their community worship, they reject the insidious inclination to play it safe. The inveterate tendency to entrenchment, which betrays itself in clinging to the tried and true, is accurately discerned as a sign of distrust in the Holy Spirit. The breath of God will not be bottled, and the gallivanting Spirit will not be campused. The worshiping ragamuffin will not be mummified in middle age by living in the past and refusing to attend to the present. Creativity and flexibility will not give way to repetition and rigidity. The ragamuffin church is comfortable with periods of silence, sitting still, listening attentively, and experiencing the divine presence. "Be still and acknowledge that I am God" (Psalm 46:10) is not merely a pious suggestion, but a divine injunction.

FOR RAGAMUFFINS, God's name is Mercy. We see our darkness as a prized possession because it drives us into the heart of God. Without mercy our darkness would plunge us into despair— and for some, self-destruction. Time alone with God reveals the unfathomable depths of the poverty of our spirit. We are so poor that even our poverty is not our own: It belongs to the *mysterium tremendum* of a loving God. In prayer we drink the dregs of this poverty. In a sudden and luminous moment we realize that we are being accosted by Mercy and embraced even before we lay hold of ourselves. Not clinging to anything, not even our sinfulness, we come before Jesus with open hands. We drain the bitter cup of self-rejection when we disappear into the tremendous poverty that is the adoration of God.

Our encounter with Mercy profoundly affects our interaction with others. "Blessed are the merciful: they shall have mercy shown them" (Matthew 5:7). We look beyond appearances, beneath surfaces, to recognize others as companions in woundedness. Human flesh is heir to the assaults, within and without, of negative, judgmental thoughts; but we will not consent to them because God is merciful to us. We will not allow these attacks to lead us into the sins of self-preoccupation and self-defense. Swimming in the merciful love of the redeeming Christ, we are free to laugh at the tendency to assume spiritual superiority—in ourselves. We are free to extend to others the mercy we have received.

Steeped in such mercy, the ragamuffin is quick to find an excuse when her neighbor is having a bad hair day, to turn aside rather than retaliate when an arrow of anger is flung her way. "Be even-tempered, content with second place, quick to forgive an offense," she remembers. "Forgive as quickly and completely as the Master forgave you. And regardless of what else you put on, wear love. It's your basic, all-purpose garment. Never be without it" (Colossians 3:13–14, *The Message).* Her example is the dying Jesus, humiliated and unjustly vilified, who cried out on behalf of His killers,

"Father, forgive them; they do not know what they are doing" (Luke 23:34).

The Big Book of Alcoholics Anonymous offers a lovely piece of homespun wisdom for those times when we are confronted with the wrongdoing of those who deliberately tried (and perhaps succeeded at) harming us:

> This was our course. We realized that the people who wronged us were perhaps spiritually sick. Though we did not like their symptoms and the way these disturbed us, they, like ourselves, were sick too. We asked God to help us show them the same tolerance, pity, and patience that we would cheerfully grant a sick friend. When a person offended, we said to ourselves, "This is a sick man. How can I be helpful to him? God, save me from being angry. Thy will be done."[3]

When you have made a slobbering mess of your life, as many of us recovering alcoholics have, compassion becomes a tad easier if you are conscientious in taking your own inventory rather than someone else's.

With a God whose name is Mercy, small wonder that gratitude surpasses every other attitude along our spiritual journey. We do not charge through life unaware of the price paid for our deliverance. Thoughtful reflection calls to mind numerous rescues and healings. "If we could count the fears, both great and small, that once hounded us, and then thank God for each dread outcome that never materialized," observed John Kavanaugh, "we would reach no end of gratitude."[4]

What infallible guarantee do we have that ragamuffins will be treated at the judgment with infinite kindness and immeasurable mercy? *Because you passed it around,* says Jesus. He stands by His Word: *Blessed are the merciful; you will be shown nothing but mercy.*

"EVERYTHING HAS been entrusted to me by [Abba]," Jesus declares, "and no one knows the Son except [Abba], just as no one knows [Abba] except the Son and those to whom the Son chooses to reveal him" (Matthew 11:27). Jesus is the Way to Abba. He is the Truth spoken by Abba. He is the Life we are invited to share—His life with Abba. "The love of God has been poured into our hearts by the Holy Spirit which has been given to us" (Romans 5:5).

The greatest gift any ragamuffin can receive from Jesus is the Abba experience. Jesus says we are to go to God with the unaffected simplicity of a child with his daddy. In a poignant psalm expressing childlike trust in God, David says, "I hold myself in quiet and silence, like a little child in its mother's arms, like a little child, so I keep myself" (Psalm 131:2). The little one is not an infant, but a weaned youngster of two or three who has been toddling around exploring the mysteries of his father's flashlight, key chain, and assorted coins left on an end table. The little ragamuffin suddenly wearies and staggers back into his mother's arms. Soothed by her affectionate words as she strokes his hair, the little guy falls asleep, tranquil and quiet.

Jesus invites us to become like a little child, to crawl into Abba's arms and let Him love on us. Though as Alan Jones notes, "The most difficult part of mature faith is to allow ourselves to be the object of God's delight."[5]

Four years ago, I attended a retreat led by an eighty-year-old biblical scholar named Frank Montalbano, who taught New Testament studies for many, many years. He focused on my favorite passage in the entire Bible, Luke 15:20. Here is how he translated it: "While he was still a long way off, his father saw him and was filled with compassion for him; he ran to his son, threw his arms around him, kissed him and could not stop kissing him." Many of us ragamuffins may be taciturn; but when it comes to accepting kisses, we are not shy.

Sitting in bold relief on a navy-blue sofa in my office is a little polka-dot rag doll. Over the last ten years, the ragamuffin mystery has laid hold of me with uncommon power. After long hours of prayer and meditation on the Scriptures and reflection on the nagging question "Who am I?" a gracious God has given me the light to see myself as I really am. I now have a primary identity and a coherent sense of myself. It affects my intimacy with God, my relationships with others, and my gentleness with myself.

Thus I want the epitaph on my tombstone to read:

BRENNAN MANNING
ABBA'S RAGAMUFFIN

Brennan Manning has served God through ministry
for nearly forty-five years. He continues to influence
others for Christ with his books and through travel and
preaching on behalf of
Willie Juan Ministries, P.O. Box 6911
New Orleans, LA 70114.

19 Mercies:
A Spiritual Journey

Welcome, Ragamuffin...

I invite you to come along on this brief journey of reading, prayer, and contemplation. Every entry in this spiritual retreat is an invitation to you to know and experience more authentically the love of Jesus Christ by the power of the Spirit. Then, once you have given Christ full possession of your heart, my prayer is that you will become His gracious presence in your world, leading others into the incomparable love of our Abba, Father.

I wish for you the awakening I experienced many years ago during a spiritual sojourn in the Saragosa Desert in Spain. One night I went to the chapel to pray. The world was asleep, but my heart was awake to the Lord and I stood at the crucifix for a long time. Then in faith, I heard Jesus Christ say, "For love of you, I left my Father's side and I came to you, who ran from Me, who fled Me, who did not want to hear My name. For love of you, I was covered with spit and punched and beaten and fixed to the wood of the cross."

I figuratively saw blood streaming from every wound and pore in Christ's body. And I heard the cry of His blood, "This isn't a joke. It is not a laughing matter to Me that I have loved you." The longer I looked, the more I realized that no man has ever loved me and no woman could ever love me as He does.

I went out into the darkness and shouted into the night, "Jesus, are You crazy? Are You out of Your mind to have loved me so much?"

The day I joined the order, an old Franciscan told me, "Once you come to experience the love of Jesus Christ, nothing else in the world will seem beautiful or desirable." That night I learned firsthand what he meant.

Therefore, my friend, in the next few pages may you receive nineteen mercies (at least!) from your loving Father. Each is an unmerited gift. Savor them deeply. Listen for the Spirit, and obey. Only then move on. You will notice that the readings are arranged in the natural sequence of a growing relationship: Come, encounter, serve, and trust.

"But Brennan," you might say, "His mercies are innumerable. They are new every morning. Why just nineteen?"

And I would reply, "Because His mercies are indeed innumerable, and all the books in the world can't contain them. And because, my fellow vagabond, these few precious mercies are enough to drench you in wonder for a lifetime and show you the Christ of your journey and heal your heart…if you let them."

O God our Father, be present with us, Your least disciples,
on each page of this journey, in each thought and emotion.
We go forward in the name of Your Son, Jesus Christ.
Lead us into the mystery of the love in the heart
of Your crucified Son, the love that surpasses all knowledge
and understanding. Cover us with His beauty. Grant us
the grace of true conversion, to make a radical break from
the darkness in our lives and move toward the Light,
who is Your Son, Jesus, who lives and reigns with You and
the Holy Spirit, one God forever and ever. Amen.

Come

1. Be here, now.

And here, at the beginning, we should begin again, don't you think? All things are new, even this by-now-familiar story.

Imagine…

You are being pursued by a ferocious tiger. You run as fast as you can but come to the edge of the cliff. Glancing back, you see the tiger about to spring. Fortunately, you also notice a rope hanging over the edge of the cliff. You grab it and scramble down, out of reach of the tiger. A close escape!

But now you look down. Five hundred feet below you see jagged rocks. So you look up. You see the tiger, crouched and waiting…and also two hungry mice, already gnawing on the rope.

What to do?

Nearby, on the face of the cliff, you notice a strawberry. Carefully, you reach out, pluck it, and eat it whole. "Yum!" you exclaim. "That's the most *delicious* strawberry I ever tasted in my whole life!"

What does this story tell us? Seize the gift of this moment! If you are preoccupied with the rocks below or the tiger above—with your past or your future—you will miss the strawberry that God wants to give you in the present moment.

In the readings ahead I ask you to make a serious effort to remain rooted in the moment. Discipline your time, your thoughts, your emotions. Don't allow anxieties or distractions to crowd out the work of the Spirit in your life. Be here now. Then the God who comes will find you in the present—waiting, listening, and ready to receive His gifts.

Reading: Psalm 139.

Calm thyself, O my soul, so that the divine can act in thee!
Calm thyself, O my soul, so that God is able to repose
in thee so that His peace may cover thee!

Søren Kierkegaard

2. Don't wait.

One of the most beautiful stories in the Gospels is of the Christ's relationship with Mary Magdalene, especially the encounter described in Luke 7. Presuming that she is the sinful woman mentioned, imagine the scene when she enters the room where Jesus and his host, Simon the Pharisee, are reclining. She—"a woman who had lived a sinful life"—hesitates before such impressive religious gathering. Clutching her alabaster jar of perfume, she starts to weep.

Perhaps you know what happened next. "Her tears fell on his feet," Luke records, "and she wiped them with her hair; then she covered his feet with kisses and anointed them with the ointment" (v. 38).

What drew Mary forward to perform her lovely act of adoration? I think she was simply overcome by the beauty and compassion of this magnetic man, Jesus! And I imagine that His eyes called out to her: Mary, come to Me. Come now. Don't wait until you get your act cleaned up and your head on straight. Don't delay until you rescue your reputation, until you're free of pride and lust, of jealousy and self-hatred. Come to Me now in your brokenness and sinfulness. Come now, with all your fears and insecurities. I will love you just the way you are—just the way you are, not the way you think you should be.

The creative power of Jesus' love called Mary Magdalene to regard herself as He did, to see in herself the possibilities which He saw in her. Mary's life stands for the central truth that through love it is possible to be delivered from the lowest depths to the shining heights where God dwells.

My friend, don't wait. Come now, simply as you are, to hear His invitation and receive His love.

Reading: Luke 7:36–38.

To adore is to recognize the whole of the object and the nothingness of the adorer. Adoration is nonentity swooning away and gladly expiring in the presence of infinity.

PERE SERTILLANGES

---

3. Jesus wants to enter into deep friendship with you.

If you grew up in Sunday school, you remember the story of Jesus calling a runt of a man named Zacchaeus down from a tree with the news, "Zacchaeus, I want to have dinner in your house today." In the Jewish tradition, to say "I want to have dinner with you" means "I want to enter into friendship with you." Even today an Orthodox Jew will not invite you to his home to dinner, unless he wants to enter into friendship or deepen an already existing friendship. It's a very sacred encounter. (That's good to recall, by the way, every time you receive communion. Jesus Christ is the Host and when He invites you to come to His table, He is declaring, "I want to enter into a deeper friendship with you.")

Zacchaeus, as you also might remember, was a greedy, dis-respected lowlife. He collected taxes for Rome from his own people and kept a kickback for himself. By his enthusiastic response to Jesus, we can guess he didn't get invited to "deeper friendship" very often! When Peter wrings his hands over Jesus' unfortunate social choice, Jesus reminds him—and us too—of His mission. He says, "I did not come to call the just.

I came to call sinners" (see Luke 19:10).

The gospel is not for the good guys with the white hats. It's for poor, weak, sinful men and women with hereditary faults and limited talents—people like you, people like me. And on Judgment Day, our lives will be measured solely in terms of our personal relationship with the risen Jesus. The Lord is going to ask each of us a question that will encompass all other questions: "Did you believe that I loved you? That I desired you? That I waited for you day after day?"

Reading: Luke 19:1–10.

May You alone enlighten me, You alone speak to me.
May all that I know apart from You be nothing more
than a chance traveling companion
on the journey toward You.

KARL RAHNER

4. Cry out for the Spirit.

Only the Spirit of Jesus Christ can accomplish the profound inner realities of a deeper faith, a real conversion of heart, a radical break with sin, a more reckless trust, a more forgiving, loving heart. So I urge you to spend time pleading for more of His Spirit and reading more of His Word.

Don't assume that the Spirit will act in your life without you taking the initiative. Cry out for a mighty outpouring of the Holy Spirit. Wherever you are—in the church or at home, alone or with others, watching television, lying in bed, or driving to work—pray continually for more of the Spirit of Jesus Christ.

Then make time to read the New Testament in private. Every day if possible, spend thirty minutes of prime time—when you're most attentive—in prayerful reading. That's when, in my experience, the Lord will speak to your heart the one word that He wants you alone to hear.

O God, I seek you, but my heart is fickle.
I believe; please help my unbelief. When all I can do
is want to want You, take my crumb of faith and break it
like bread to feed thousands, beginning, by Your mercy,
with me. You reject no desperate, sinful, seeking child.
You say only and always, Come! I come to You, God.
Pour out Your Spirit on me.
Speak Your words of life to this child.
I pray in Jesus' name, amen.

Encounter

5. The Person of Jesus.

Who is this Jesus of Nazareth—this Nazarene carpenter in whose name vast theological systems have been developed, worldwide churches organized, crusades, reforms, and renewals launched?

Church councils have rendered their opinions, as have historians, theologians, emperors, film directors, and all manner of believers and doubters.

But other people cannot answer on our behalf. You must answer and respond for yourself. So must I. Jesus put the question to His own disciples:

"But what about you?" He asked. "Who do you say I am?"

Peter answered, "You are the Christ" (Mark 8:29).

My companion of the road, I ask you: Describe the Christ that you have personally encountered on the grounds of your own self. Describe Him as you would to a friend over coffee. Describe not the diety you have heard about or been taught to believe exists, but only the Christ you have actually encountered.

And then, I invite you to reflect soberly on what your own answer reveals to you.

Reading: Mark 8:27–30; Romans 10:8–13.

I pray that out of his glorious riches he may strengthen
you with power through his Spirit in your inner being,

so that Christ may dwell in your hearts through faith.
And I pray that you, being rooted and established in love,
may have power...to grasp how wide and long and high
and deep is the love of Christ, and to know this love
that surpasses knowledge—that you may be filled
to the measure of all the fullness of God.

THE APOSTLE PAUL

6. The call from the cross.

Receiving the Person of Jesus into every corner of our lives as the Christ is the beginning of a ragamuffin's transformation. But our transformation springs from an absurd fact: this Jesus of our journey is a crucified God. Yes, the message of the Cross is complete absurdity for those who are headed for ruin. But to us who are experiencing salvation, unaccountably, it is both the power and the unsearchable wisdom of God.

The passion of Jesus is an ugly fact in history. But if we are to continue throughout our lives to drink of the life-giving water of the Holy Spirit, we must continue to draw near to the body of our crucified Lord from whom the saving waters flow. Union with Jesus in the mystery of His passion and death is the indispensable condition for experiencing the power and the wisdom of God in our lives. This is what Paul gets at when he writes in Philippians, "I want to know Christ and the power of his resurrection and the fellowship of sharing in his sufferings, becoming like him in his death" (Philippians 3:10). The day that we cease proclaiming Jesus Christ nailed to the cross is the day we effectively part company with the gospel.

And the call to every disciple is also to the cross. Paul told the Galatians, "You cannot belong to Christ Jesus unless you crucify all self-indulgent desires and passions" (see Galatians 5:16–15). Self-mastery over every form of sin, selfishness, emotional dishonesty, and degraded love is the less-traveled road to Christian freedom. But there is no growth without pain and no integrity without self-denial. (Of course, neither pursuit is particularly attractive apart from the personal love of Jesus Christ.)

Listen to what Jesus speaks to you from the cross: "I'm dying to be with you. I'm really dying to be with you."

And then He whispers, "Will you die a little to be with Me?"

Reading: 1 Corinthians 1:18–2:5; Philippians 3:7–11.

> *No one, it seems to me, who has fully grasped*
> *the Crucifixion can ever again take seriously*
> *any expression or instrument of worldly power,*
> *however venerable, glittering, or seemingly formidable.*
>
> MALCOLM MUGGERIDGE

---

7. Through Jesus we know Abba.

Who is the God of your imagination—really? Is He the invisible honorary president of outer space? A Great Hangman in the sky? The policeman who bats you over the head with his nightstick every time you stumble and fall? The niggling customs officer rifling through your moral suitcase looking for your good deeds and bad? The omnipotent thug who invades to rob you of peace and joy?

All these are common human projections. By projection, I mean that we are imposing on God our own impoverished understanding of Him. What a costly deception! To pray to any God other than a Father who finds sheer delight in reconciliation is illusion, cowardice, and superstition. Worse, it is idolatry.

The true God is no other than the One we see in the person of Jesus. Jesus came to make the invisible God both visible and audible—"Anyone who has seen me has seen the Father," he said (John 14:9). You want to know what your heavenly Father is like? Look into the eyes of Jesus. Jesus Christ alone shows us the full and astonishing revelation of the Father. Jesus is the human face of God.

One day, the disciples asked Jesus, "Lord, teach us to pray."
Jesus replied, "When you pray, you are to say, 'Our Father...'"
Our Father.

Familiar words to us, certainly. But to the twelve apostles, revolutionary words never heard by prophets and priests who had come before. In that revelation of Jesus, all the false images of God are blown away.

Do you believe that God is your Father, or do you still find that news too good to be true?

Reading: John 14:6–11.

Be thou my vision, O Lord of my heart,
Naught is all else to me, save that thou art.
Thou my best thought by day and by night,

Waking or sleeping, thy presence my light.
Be thou my wisdom, thou my true word;
I ever with thee, thou with me, Lord.

EIGHTH-CENTURY IRISH PRAYER

8. The God who is love.

A second radical message from Jesus about the Father is that God is love. It sounds almost trite, doesn't it? But a comparative study of world religions will show how striking and novel is the Christian affirmation that God is love.

That means that all God does is love. Not only that God is love, but that God is loving—in fact, that He always acts in a loving way. Just as the sun only shines, conferring its light and warmth on those who will receive them, so God only loves, shedding His light and warmth on those who would receive them.

All changes in the quality of a Christian's life grow out of a change in one's vision of reality. Jesus said, "You will come to know the truth, and the truth will set you free" (John 8:32).

Therefore, I ask you: Do you really believe that God is unchangeably, unalterably loving? And have you let that change your personal vision of reality…every hidden corner and embarrassing shadow and intense desire of it? Your personal transformation begins here.

When I was a little boy I had a naïve idea that when I went to confession, God was frowning on me because I had been bad. As soon as I confessed my sins, God would begin to smile again. Somehow my confession implied a change in God. How absurd! My confession only implies a change in me.

Now I understand things differently. More like this: You and I are standing in the middle of a spotlight on the platform of a church; the rest of the church is in darkness, but we are in bright light. To me this scene is a good image of ragamuffins living in a state of grace. Now, suppose that you or I commit grave, deliberate sin. What happens? We step aside into shadows, but the light remains shining. God's love never changes—we have simply chosen to step away from it. When we repent, we come back into the light of God's love, which has always been there.

Reading: 1 John 4:7–16.

Grace is the majesty, the freedom,
the undeservedness, the unexpectedness, the newness,
the arbitrariness, in which a relationship to God and
therefore the possibility of knowing Him is opened up to
man by God Himself… Grace is God's good pleasure.

KARL BARTH

9. God loves you unconditionally.

Finally, the astonishing revelation of Jesus about His Father reveals that you and I are loved by God unconditionally and as we are.

Think about this with me. Your Father God loves you as you are, not as you should be. He loves you beyond fidelity and infidelity, beyond worthiness and unworthiness. He loves you in the

morning sun and the evening rain. He loves you equally in your
state of grace and in your state of disgrace. He loves you without
caution, regret, boundary, limit, breaking point. No matter what
happens or what you do…He can't stop loving you!

Once I was about to leave on a trip to New York City with
two friends, Paul and Jenny. Paul, a banker who had business in
the city, had invited his wife along. But at their house just before
we were to leave for the airport, their three-year-old, Marie,
unexpectedly spiked a mild fever.

Jenny turned to Paul. "We can't go to New York," she said.

Paul tried to be reassuring. "Jenny, she's had that twice the
past year," he pleaded. "Her temperature goes up a little, then
in a few hours it goes back to normal. Besides, my parents are
here to look after her—remember? Let's go!" Reluctantly, Jenny
agreed and we left for the airport.

Now, this is what I remember most about that trip:

We're still in the car on the way to the airport when Paul
said, "Honey, just think, tonight we're going to stay at the Plaza
Hotel!"

"Oh, that's beautiful!" Jenny replied. "We haven't been
there since our honeymoon. And as soon as I get to the airport,
I'll call home and see how Marie is doing."

A few minutes later Paul said, "And honey, tomorrow night
we're going to go see the play *Chicago*! Then we're going to
Sardi's for dinner."

"Oh, I've read in *Gourmet* magazine that if you go to
Sardi's, you gotta have their filet of beef," said Jenny. "That's
what I'll have. And I can call home every night from the Plaza
and see how Marie is doing."

Nine times in the next twenty minutes, Jenny Sheldon spontaneously brought her concern for her daughter's welfare into the conversation—and we hadn't even left town yet!

Listen, my brother and sister, Jesus Christ came to tell us that it is more likely that Jenny Sheldon would forget her baby Marie than that God could ever forget you! If you took the love of all the best mothers and fathers who ever lived (think about that for a moment)—all the goodness, kindness, patience, fidelity, wisdom, tenderness, strength, and love—and united all those virtues in one person, that person would only be a faint shadow of the love and the mercy in the heart of God for you and me.

Reading: Isaiah 49:15–16; Luke 15:11–33.

The great spiritual battle begins—and never ends—with the reclaiming of our chosenness. Long before any human being saw us, we are seen by God's loving eyes. Long before anyone heard us cry or laugh, we are heard by our God who is all ears for us. Long before any person spoke to us in this world, we are spoken to by the voice of eternal love. Our preciousness, uniqueness, and individuality are not given to us by those who meet us in clock-time—our brief chronological existence—but by the One who has chosen us with an everlasting love, a love that existed from all eternity and will last through all eternity.

HENRI J. M. NOUWEN

10. We cry, "Abba!"

A rabbi invited me to a bar mitzvah at his synagogue. During dinner I watched as the rabbi's four-year-old son finished what he had to eat, got bored, and wandered away from the table. But he hadn't gone far before the little boy suddenly seemed to his bearings. Turning around in a panic, he searched until he spotted his father at the head of the table. Then he ran as fast as his little legs would carry him. Two feet from the table, he flung himself into his father's lap shouting, "Ab…Ab…Abba!"

Even today, *Abba* is the first word most Israeli children learn—Abba! Daddy!

Jesus says that is the true posture of Christian prayer—that of a little child, fleeing to his father's lap, calling, "Daddy! Daddy!" During those crushing hours in the Garden, Jesus cried out, "Abba, Father…!" (Mark 14:36). And the apostle Paul reminds us that all God's sons and daughters have received the same Spirit, "enabling us to cry out, 'Abba, Father!'" (Romans 8:15).

Do you see why the revelation of Jesus on the nature of God is so revolutionary? Why no Christian can ever say one form of prayer is as good as another, or one religion is as good as another? What Jesus Christ reveals is that the God in whose presence Moses had to remove his shoes, the God from whose fingertips this universe fell, the God beside whose grandeur the Grand Canyon is only a glimpse, the God besides whose power the nuclear bomb is as nothing—this infinite, holy God, Jesus announces, we may dare to address with intimacy. With the same tenderness, familiarity, and reverence, in fact, as a toddler flying to his father's lap while calling out, "Da...Da...Daddy!"

Reading: Galatians 3:26-4:7.

We make ourselves what we are
by the way we address God.

THOMAS MERTON

11. The prayer of simple regard.

You don't have to enter a Trappist monastery or go to the desert to learn contemplative prayer. Begin here: Spend forty minutes a day of prime time simply and reverently praying, "Abba...I belong to you."

When you inhale, say, "Abba."

When you exhale, "I belong to you." The prayer is exactly seven syllables, and corresponds perfectly with the normal rhythm of our breathing. In three months, you will have arrived at the prayer of simple regard.

You can pray this prayer watching television, lying in bed, driving to work, eating dinner, sitting here in the chapel. I often pray it while I preach.

Abba...I belong to you.

Abba...I belong to you.

Abba...I belong to you.

This simple utterance of adoration and submission infuses our being with a profound awareness of who we are—a son or daughter of the Father in Christ Jesus by the power of the Holy Spirit. And by affirming that over and over through our day, we also receive a sense of why we're here, and where we are going.

> *Lord Jesus, be for me the way to Abba, Father.*
> *Be for me all my truth and all my life. Lead me into*
> *the crucified life, which is real life, and eternal. Lead me*
> *away from every lesser thing. By Your love, renew my inner*
> *being so that I can receive Your love, and know it truly,*
> *and be Your love to others. Amen.*

Serve

12. The freedom of serving.

What image comes to your mind when you think of the return of Jesus Christ in glory? In Luke we read Jesus' own testimony that when He returns in glory, He will come as a servant of the people of God. "Blessed those servants whom the master finds awake when he comes," we read. "In truth I tell you, He will do up his belt, sit them down at table and wait on them" (Luke 12:37).

This unprecedented and scandalous reversal of the world's values—a triumphant Messiah who comes to serve—shows Christians the way to joyful freedom in serving:

- in sovereign liberty to prefer to be the servant, rather than the lord of the household;

- to merrily taunt the gods of power, prestige, honor, and recognition;
- to refuse to take oneself seriously, and for that matter, to refuse to take seriously anyone else who takes themselves seriously;
- to be captivated with joy and wonder at the vision and lifestyle of Jesus, servant of God...

These revolutionary attitudes of compassion and selflessness bear the stamp of genuine discipleship. But we should never mistake them with watery-eyed sentimentality. Compassion is a spirituality of meat, not milk; of love, not masochism; of justice, not philanthropy. It requires maturity, a big heart, a willingness to risk, and imagination. The unglamorous and little-noticed works of mercy, feeding and sheltering, visiting the sick and incarcerated, educating, correcting, encouragement, bearing wrongs, counseling, comforting and praying with people embody the kingdom lifestyle.

Personally, my friend, I would rather be numbered among the ragged few who learn joyful service from Jesus than among the legalizers, moralizers, and hairsplitters who build monuments of religious correctness...then cannot see over them to a child of God in need.

Reading: Galatians 5.

People are hungry for God.
People are hungry for love. Are you aware of that?
Do you know that? Do you see that?
Do you have eyes to see?

Quite often we look but we don't see.
We are all passing through this world.
We need to open our eyes and see.

MOTHER TERESA

13. Healing through meal sharing.

Christian servanthood is not an emotion or a state of mind. It is a decision to live the life of Jesus. It has nothing to do with what we feel, and everything to do with what we do.

Reflecting again on Jesus' meal with Zacchaeus (that pint-size scammer and scoundrel), we must realize that we can scarcely appreciate the scandal that Jesus Christ caused. In first-century Judaism, table fellowship with beggars, tax collectors, and prostitutes was a religious, social, and cultural taboo. And it did not escape the Pharisees' attention that Jesus actually intended to befriend Zacchaeus! He was not only breaking the law; He was rejecting the very structure of Jewish society.

Now try to imagine the impact of these meals from the point of view of Zacchaeus and others of his lowly ilk. By accepting them as friends and equals, Jesus took away their shame, humiliation, and guilt. By sharing bread with them, He proved to them that they mattered to Him first as people. By caring conversation, He restored their dignity and released them from old captivities.

How, my friend, are we to personally respond to these dramatic social choices of our Lord? This I propose:

That we also must consider the healing power of a meal shared.

That we should welcome sinners into our community of salvation.

That, with merry abandon, we must in every way possible scatter abroad the indiscriminate love of God.

Reading: Luke 5:27–32; Romans 12:9–16.

God loves what in us is not yet. What has still to come to birth.
What we love in a person is what already is:
virtue, beauty, courage, and hence our love is self-interested
and fragile. God, loving what is not yet and putting faith in us,
continually begets us, since love is what begets.
By giving us confidence, God helps us to be born,
since love is what helps us emerge from our darkness and
draws us to the light. And this is such a fine thing to do
that God invites us to do the same.

CARLO CARRETTO

14. Washing feet.

One morning at a retreat center, I was reading the passage in John 13 that describes Jesus washing the feet of His disciples when I was suddenly transported in faith to the Upper Room. And there I took Judas's place.

The Servant Jesus had just tied a towel around His waist and poured water from a pitcher into a copper basin. He reached out to wash my feet. Involuntarily, I pulled back. I couldn't even look at Him. I knew in my heart that I betrayed His vision, been unfaithful to my dream and thus unfaithful to His plan for my life.

But Jesus placed His hand on my knee and said, "Brennan, do you know what these years together have meant to me? You were being held, even when you didn't believe I was holding you. I love you, my friend."

Tears flowed down my cheeks. "But, Lord, my sins, my repeated failures, my weaknesses," I protested.

"I understand," He said. "Brennan, I expected more failure from you than you expected from yourself." He smiled, then said, "You always came back. Nothing pleases me so much as when you trust Me, when you allow My compassion to be greater than your sinfulness."

"But, Jesus," I blurted, "my irritating character defects, the boasting, the inflating the truth, the pretenses, the impatience, all the times I got drunk…"

"What you're saying is true, Brennan. Yet your love for Me never wavered and your heart remained pure. And besides, you've done one thing that makes Me forget all the rest."

I leaned forward, bewildered. "What?" I asked.

Jesus answered, "You've been kind to sinners…."

I sobbed so hard that the priest in the next room at the retreat came over and rapped on my door to see if anything was wrong. I assured him that I was okay, and I returned to prayer.

Then I heard Jesus say, "Now I'll go. I just washed your feet. Do the same for others. Serve My people humbly and lovingly. You will find happiness if you do. Peace, My friend."

Reading: John 13:1–17.

*Why have You kindled in me the flame of faith, this dark light
which lures us out of the bright security of our little huts into
Your night? And why have You made me Your priest, one whose
vocation it is to be with You on behalf of men, when my
finiteness makes me gasp for breath in Your presence?*

KARL RAHNER

15. Freedom from your own contempt.

Self-hatred is an enormous obstacle to loving other people.
Usually we dislike others not because we love ourselves too
much, but because we're not able to love ourselves enough. We
fear and distrust others because we feel inadequate. We hide
behind anger, sarcasm, or judgmentalism because we're convinced that we don't measure up ourselves.

Interestingly, you can read the Gospels line by line and
find that Jesus devoted not one minute of His ministry to
reinforcing negative self-concepts. By contrast, much con-
ventional Christianity says that we should look in the mirror
every morning and exclaim, "Worm! Maggot! You despicable
wretch!"

That is not the gospel of Jesus Christ. He said, "Love your
neighbor as yourself." In other words, my capacity to love you
lies in direct proportion to my ability to love myself. Father

Adrian von Kahn has written, "Gentleness toward my precious, fragile self as called forth uniquely by God constitutes the core of my gentleness with others, and it is also the main condition for my presence to God."

My friend, do you ever allow yourself to believe that Jesus appreciates you for wanting Him? For wanting to say no to so many things that would separate you from Him? Do you ever permit yourself to think that Jesus is grateful to you for giving comfort to another person? For pausing to smile at one of His children who has such a great need to see a smile? For learning more about Him? Do you ever think that Jesus can be saddened and disappointed in you for not believing that He has forgiven you totally?

The mystery of our faith is this: God loves us and Jesus Christ would have died for us, even if we had been the only person on earth. Paul Tillich never tired of saying, "Faith is the courage to accept acceptance, to accept that God loves me as I am and not as I should be, because I'm never going to be as I should be."

The gospel of Jesus Christ calls us to recognize our intrinsic worth and dignity, to love ourselves humbly and wholesomely, and to forgive ourselves as we have been forgiven. Anything less is a refusal to accept God's love for us. In fact, it is a rejection of Christ's death on the cross for us as a colossal blunder.

Consider this: If Jesus sat at your dining room table tonight and laid out your whole life story—the miserable, recurring sins, the hidden agenda, the skeletons in the closet, the dark desires unknown even to yourself—you would still experience joy, peace, and acceptance in His presence.

Why? Because you would finally recognize the being of inestimable value that Jesus sees in you. And because you would hear Him say, "Your sins go over here. It's you that I've come for, My friend."

Reading: Psalm 51.

If the Lord Jesus Christ has washed you in
His own blood
and forgiven you all your sins,
how dare you refuse to forgive yourself?

FRANCIS McNUTT

16. Christ in the person next to you.

In the winter of 1947, the Abbey Pierre, a modern apostle of mercy to the poor of Paris, found a young family on the streets homeless, almost frozen to death. He scooped them up and brought them back to his little dwelling, which was already filled with other vagrants. He had no place to put them, so the Abbey Pierre went into the chapel, removed the blessed sacrament from the tabernacle, placed it upstairs in a cold, unheated attic, and then installed the family in the chapel to sleep. When his Dominican brothers expressed shock at such irreverence toward the blessed sacrament, the Abbey Pierre replied, "Jesus Christ is not cold in the Eucharist, but He is cold in the body of a little child."

Every time we come together to celebrate the Eucharist, we

readily believe that at the words of consecration, Jesus Christ is really and truly present in the bread. Why do we believe that? Because He said it: "This is my body."

But He also said that He's present in those around us. "What you did for those in need, what you did to the very least of your brothers and sisters, that's what you did to Me. And that's how much you loved Me." Why don't we believe that?

Mother Teresa expressed so powerfully, by her life and her words, how she saw the world and Christ in it. "In the Eucharist I see Christ in the appearance of the bread," she wrote. "In the slums, I see Christ in the distressing disguise of the poor. The Eucharist and the poor are but one love for me."

Right now, the Lord is in the person next to you, in front of you, behind you. When you go home tonight and open the door of your home, the Lord will be present in each person there. Sometimes He's buried there. Sometimes He's bound hand and foot there, but He's there. And you and I, my friend, have been given the gift of faith to detect His presence there, and the Holy Spirit has been poured out into our hearts that we might love Him there, because the meaning of our religion is love.

Lord Jesus, Savior, Servant…help me to dream again.
Rekindle in my heart that fire of the disciple who sees
his calling everywhere, hears Your invitation everywhere,
reaches out to Your children in great need…everywhere.
I really do want to live Your life in mine—to serve, to care,
to give, to sing Your song—for Your glory and pleasure.
Amen.

Trust

17. Trust in your Father's delight.

The Trappist monk Basil Pennington captures the simplicity of prayer when he writes: "A father is delighted when his little one, leaving off his toys and friends, runs to him and climbs into his arms. As he hold his little one close to him, he cares little whether the child is looking around, his attention flitting from one thing to another, or if he's intent upon his father, or just settling down to sleep. The father doesn't care, because essentially the child is choosing to be with his father, confident of the love, the care, the security that is his in those arms."

All prayer should be just like that. As sons and daughters of the new covenant, we are given immediate access to the Father's lap. We settle down in our Father's arms and His loving hands. Our minds, our thoughts, our imagination may flit about here and there. We might even fall asleep. But essentially we are choosing to remain for this time intimately with our Father— giving ourselves to Him, receiving His love and care, letting Him enjoy us as He will.

Of course, our inclination usually is to bring to prayer only what we're comfortable with. But the more we dare to reveal our whole trembling self to Him with all our anxieties, dark desires, fears, sensuality, laziness, and incompetence, the more we'll be able to experience His compassionate caring, which is perfect love that will cast out all our fears.

Reading: Psalm 131; 1 John 3:1.

Blessed be the God and Father of our Lord Jesus Christ. Before the world was made, He chose us in Christ to be holy and spotless, to live through love in His presence, determining that we should become His adopted sons through Jesus Christ.

THE APOSTLE PAUL

18. Worry is an insult to your Father.

Charles de Foucauld, the found of the Little Brothers of Jesus, wrote a single sentence that's had a profound impact on my life. He said, "The one thing we owe absolutely to God is never to be afraid of anything." Never to be afraid of anything, even death, which, after all, is but that final breakthrough into the open, waiting, outstretched arms of Abba.

"There is no need to be afraid, little flock," Jesus said, "for it has pleased your father to give you the kingdom" (Luke 12:32). As a bumper sticker I saw in Texas read, "Worry is an insult to your Father."

You remember how Jesus prayed during His moment of crisis in Gethsemane? Almost hysterical with fear and terror at the fate that lay ahead of Him, with beads of sweat turning to drops of blood, He cried out, "'Abba, Father!' he said, 'For you everything is possible. Take this cup away from me. But let it be as you, not I, would have it'" (Mark 14:36).

When I woke up this morning, I propped a second pillow under my head and I lay in bed for quite a while, just pray-

ing, "Abba, I belong to you." Every word helped me to center
on my primary identity, and to establish a coherent sense of self.
It was like stepping into a hot bath—just letting the Father's
love seep in, saturate, permeate every part of my being.

I long for you to let go of worry and allow yourself to trust
God completely. It's one thing to know your Father loves you
and quite another thing to experience it.

Reading: Matthew 6:25–34; John 14:1–7.

I wonder if fear is not our main obstacle to prayer.
When we enter into the presence of God and start to sense
the huge reservoir of fear inside us, we want to run away
into the many distractions, which our busy world offers
so abundantly. But we shouldn't be afraid of our fears.
We can confront them, give words to them and
lead them into the presence of the One who says,
"Be not afraid. It is I."

HENRI J. M. NOUWEN

19. The grace of reckless love.

Finally, I invite you to return to that scene of mercy I mentioned at the beginning—a room intoxicated by perfume. Jesus,
reclining, is teaching, listening, and answering questions.
Simon, the Pharisee, and all the other important people on
guest list are straining to understand. And through it all, the fra-
grance of Mary's love pervades the room.

At last Jesus turns toward the woman at His feet, but addresses Simon:

> "You see this woman? I came into your house, and you poured no water over my feet, but she poured out her tears over my feet and wiped them away with her hair. You gave me no kiss, but she has been covering my feet with kisses ever since I came in. You did not anoint my head with oil, but she has anointed my feet with ointment."

Then Jesus says something about Mary Magdalene that, as far as we know, He never said to anyone else:

> "I tell you that her sins, many as they are, have been forgiven her, because she has shown such great love. It is someone who is forgiven little that shows little love." (Luke 7:44–47)

You know, Mary Magdalene would have been buried in history as an unknown hooker, except for this—her reckless, passionate, uncompromising love for the Person of Jesus.

Is your relationship with Jesus marked by reckless love? Authentic Christianity, according to the Word, is this: It's the thrill, the excitement, of falling in love with the risen, living Jesus Christ. He shows us the way to the Father, He pours out on us the Spirit of Pentecost—not so that we'll be nicer people with better morals, but brand-new creations, human torches ignited with the flaming Spirit of the living God.

Oh, God, my Father, thank You for Your mercies—
innumerable, measureless, fathomless… Thank You!
Be present with me now on each step of this ragamuffin
journey. Grow me up in my inner being to receive and
share abroad more and more of Your love. Let me be Your
hands and face and words to all I meet. Set me free to
serve You—free from anxiety, fear, self-pity, self-hatred,
cynicism, or skepticism. Free me from every crippling sin
and any darkness of unbelief. Lord Jesus Christ, anoint
my life and my spiritual community with deep faith
and reckless abandonment to Your enduring goodness.
Give us truly listening hearts, that we may hear Your Word
and courageously act upon it, to the praise of Your name
and joy of Your heart. I ask this in the name of Your Son,
our Lord Jesus Christ. Amen.

Notes

Chapter 1

1. Eugene O'Neill, *The Great God Brown* (1926).
2. Anthony De Mello, *Taking Flight: A Book of Story Meditations* (New York: Doubleday, 1988), 105.
3. Fyodor Dostoyevsky, *Crime and Punishment,* trans. Constance Garnett (New York: Random House, 1950), 322.
4. Jaroslav Pelikan, *Jesus Through the Centuries: His Place in the History of Culture* (New Haven, CT: Yale University Press, 1985), 158. This is a work of vast and carefully concealed scholarship which traces the images of Jesus from New Testament times down to the twentieth century. Pelikan suggests that the way a particular age depicted Jesus is an essential key to understanding that age. The later chapters of the book show that "as respect for the organized church has declined, reverence for Jesus has grown."
5. Robert Farrar Capon, *Between Noon and Three* (San Francisco: Harper & Row, 1982), 114–15, quoted in Donald W. McCullough, *Waking from the American Dream* (Downers Grove, IL: InterVarsity Press, 1988), 205.

6. De Mello, 113–14.

7. Marcus S. Borg, *Jesus, A New Vision: Spirit, Culture, and the Life of Discipleship* (New York: Harper & Row, 1987), 35.

8. Paul Tillich, *The Shaking of the Foundations* (New York: Scribner's, 1948), 161–62.

9. Hans Küng, *On Being a Christian* (New York: Doubleday, 1976), 507–8. Küng is one of those rare thinkers incapable of superficial thought. I find it difficult to state without hyperbole the value and importance of this book in my life.

Chapter 2

1. This fascinating collection of scientific data was drawn from a Rotary Club presentation in Sea Island, Georgia, in 1978. The speaker's name is not available to me at this time.

2. Peter van Breemen, *Certain As the Dawn* (Denville, NJ: Dimension Books, 1980), 13.

3. Walter J. Burghardt, *Grace on Crutches: Homilies for Fellow Travelers* (New York: Paulist Press, 1985), 101–2.

4. Ibid., 108.

5. Flannery O'Connor, *The Complete Stories* (New York: Farrar, Straus and Giroux, 1971), 491. The author (1925–1964) died of incurable lupus and left behind a body of fiction, especially short stories, that rank as Christian classics. Before her death she said, "You will have found Christ when you are concerned with other people's sufferings and not your own."

6. Gerhard Ebeling, *Luther: An Introduction to His Thought* (Philadelphia: Fortress Press, 1970), 45–46.

7. Mary Jane Frances Cavolina, Maureen Anne Teresa Kelly, Jeffrey Allen Joseph Stone, Richard Glen Michael Davis, *Growing Up Catholic* (New York: Doubleday, 1984), 15–16.

8. Van Breemen, 61.

Chapter 3

1. Donald P. Gray, *Jesus: The Way to Freedom* (Winona, MN: St. Mary's College, 1979), 38. This little seventy-two-page jewel is scholarly yet eminently readable. It breathes the air of the gospel of grace. Gray's vision of Jesus is like refreshing rain falling on parched earth. Highly recommended.

2. Simon Tugwell, *The Beatitudes: Soundings in Christian Traditions* (Springfield, IL: Templegate, 1980), 7. In my opinion, of the scores of books written on the Beatitudes, none have matched the depth and wisdom of Tugwell's book.

3. Albert Nolan, *Jesus Before Christianity* (Maryknoll, NY: Orbis Books, 1978), 56. Nolan presents a portrait of Jesus before He became enshrined in doctrines, dogma, and ritual. A valuable and compelling little work.

4. Ibid., 23.

5. Brennan Manning, *A Stranger to Self-Hatred* (Denville, NJ: Dimension Books, 1983), 47.

6. Nolan, 39.

7. Nolan, 56.

8. Edward Schillebeeckx, *Jesus: An Experiment in Christology* (New York: Seabury Press, 1976), 165.

9. Walter Kasper, *Jesus the Christ* (New York: Paulist Press, 1977), 86. I found the author's prose heavy and the style ingratiating, but a careful reading reaps rich rewards.

10. Robert C. Frost, *Our Heavenly Father* (Plainfield, NJ: Logos International, 1978), 44. Frost credibly and imaginatively reconstructs the hidden life of Jesus before He began His public ministry. Recommended for Bible study and small group discussion.

11. Burghardt, 144.

12. Gerald S. Sloyan, *Jesus in Focus: A Life in Its Setting* (Mystic, CT: Twenty-Third Publications, 1986), 38.

13. William Shakespeare, *Macbeth* (1605), act V, scene 5.

Chapter 4

1. De Mello, 114–15.
2. Gray, 33.
3. Ibid., 19.
4. Eugene Kennedy, *The Choice to Be Human* (New York: Doubleday, 1985), 128.
5. Donald W. McCullough, *Waking from the American Dream* (Downers Grove, IL: InterVarsity Press, 1988), 116. The spirit of his book permeates the pages of mine, especially his chapter "The Difference Friday Makes." I am indebted to Dr. McCullough and understand why Richard Halverson, the chaplain of the U.S. Senate, wrote, "This book is imperative reading for all who take Christ seriously."
6. Peter van Breemen, *As Bread That Is Broken,* (Denville, NJ: Dimension Books, 1975), 196.
7. Gerald G. May, *Addiction and Grace* (San Francisco: Harper & Row, 1988), 166. This book broadens our understanding of addiction (which can range from cocaine to an idea) and the gentle interplay of grace in regaining our freedom.
8. De Mello, 74.

Chapter 5

1. Joan Puls, *A Spirituality of Compassion* (Mystic, CT: Twenty-Third Publications, 1988), 119–20.
2. Sean Caulfield, *The God of Ordinary People* (Kansas City, MO: Sheed and Ward, 1988), 50.
3. Puls, 120.
4. Molière, *Don Juan* (1665).
5. James N. McCutcheon, "The Righteous and the Good," in

Best Sermons (San Francisco: Harper & Row, 1988), 238–39.

6. Frederick Buechner, *The Magnificent Defeat* (San Francisco: Harper & Row, 1985), 47.

7. Andrew M. Greeley, *God in Popular Culture* (Chicago, IL: Thomas More Press, 1988), 124.

8. Peter S. Hawkins, *The Language of Grace* (Cambridge, MA: Cowley Publications, 1983), 67–68. The author examines the fiction of Flannery O'Connor, Walker Percy, and Irish Murdock and examines the language of grace they employ to confront the modern reader on the premise that many of the traditional words on grace have been devalued.

9. Walter J. Burghardt, *Still Proclaiming Your Wonders* (New York: Paulist Press, 1984), 170.

10. Brennan Manning, *Prophets and Lovers* (Denville, NJ: Dimension Books, 1976), 12–14. Here I have condensed a broad biblical theology of divine agape from one of my previously published works.

Chapter 6

1. Richard Selzer, MD, *Mortal Lessons: Notes on the Art of Surgery* (New York: Simon and Shuster, 1978), 45–46. I first read this story in *The Wittenburg Door,* an often satirical Christian magazine that advertises itself as "the perfect gift for the closed mind." I always await the next issue with considerable anticipation.

2. Jürgen Moltmann, *The Crucified God* (New York: Harper & Row, 1974), 108.

3. Joachim Jeremias, *The Parables of Jesus* (New York: Charles Scribner's Sons, 1970), 72.

4. Ibid., 188.

5. Tugwell, 23.

6. John Shea, *Stories of God* (Chicago, IL: Thomas More Press, 1978), 187. One of the most original and creative thinkers in

the American church today.

7. McCullough, 122.

8. John R. Claypool, "Learning to Forgive Ourselves," in *Best Sermons 1* (San Francisco: Harper & Row, 1988), 269.

9. Quote from St. Francis de Sales. Source unknown.

10. Walter J. Burghardt, *Tell the Next Generation* (New York: Paulist Press, 1980), 43.

11. Jon Sobrino, *Christology at the Crossroads: A Latin American Approach* (Maryknoll, NY: Orbis Books, 1978), 171.

12. Burghardt, *Grace on Crutches,* 43.

Chapter 7

1. I have developed this true account in a different fashion in my *Gentle Revolutionaries.*

2. Dietrich Bonhoeffer, *Life Together* (San Francisco: Harper & Row, 1954), quoted in Bob and Michael Benson, *Disciplines for the Inner Life* (Waco, TX: Word Books, 1985), 60. A helpful little book of guided Scripture readings coupled with the writings of spiritual leaders in order to deepen the inner life.

3. C. S. Lewis, *The Problem of Pain* (New York: Macmillan), 49–50.

4. Anthony De Mello, *The Song of the Bird* (Anand, India: Gujaret Sahitya Prakash, distributed by Chicago: Loyola University Press, 1983), 130.

5. Kennedy, 8–9. Kennedy's book, subtitled *Jesus Alive in the Gospel of Matthew,* ranks among the best books I have read in the past ten years.

6. May, 169.

Chapter 8

1. Hans Küng, *Freedom Today* (New York: Sheed and Ward, 1966), 36–37. The passage from *The Brothers Karamazov* was cited here.

2. Brother Roger, *Parable of Community* (Minneapolis, MN: Seabury Press, 1980), 4.

3. Henri J. M. Nouwen, *Lifesigns, Intimacy, Fecundity, and Ecstasy in Christian Perspective* (New York: Doubleday, 1986), 38. A fine little book offering the essential key to a life free from the domination of fear.

4. Gray, 45.

5. William Kilpatrick, *Identity and Intimacy* (New York: Sheed and Ward, 1975), 112.

6. Carl J. Jung, *Modern Man in Search of a Soul* (Harcourt, Brace and World Harvest Books, 1933), 235.

7. M. Basil Pennington, *Centering Prayer: Renewing an Ancient Christian Prayer Form* (Garden City, NY: Doubleday, 1980), 68–69. The great value of this book lies in the simplicity and clarity of the presentation. A way of praying that leads to a deep, living relationship with God.

8. Anthony De Mello, *The Heart of the Enlightened* (New York: Doubleday, 1989), 122.

9. John L. McKenzie, *Source: What the Bible Says About the Problems of Contemporary Life* (Chicago: Thomas More Press, 1984), 146.

10. Küng, *Freedom Today.*

11. Fyodor Dostoyevsky, *The Brothers Karamozov* (New York: Modern Library, Random House, 1934), 272. One of the most enduring masterpieces ever written with the opening inscription, "I tell you most solemnly, unless a grain of wheat falls on the ground and dies, it remains only a single grain; but if it dies, it yields a rich harvest" (John 12:24).

Chapter 9

1. Gerald O'Collins, *The Second Journey: Spiritual Awareness and the Mid-Life Crisis* (New York: Paulist Press, 1978), 4. This book offers a compassionate insight into the anxiety and inner turmoil that often accompanies the crisis of the middle years. It is encouraging to read the stories of others who have walked this well-trod path.
2. Ibid., 62.
3. Brennan Manning, *Souvenirs of Solitude* (Denville, NJ: Dimension Books, 1979), 8–28. Here, I drew material from a previous work of mine now out of print.
4. Nikos Kazantzakis, *Report to Greco* (London: Faber and Faber, 1973).

Chapter 10

1. *Love and Death*, screenplay by Woody Allen (Jack Rollins & Charles H. Joffe Productions, distributed by United Artists, 1975).
2. Russell Baker, *Growing Up* (New York: Signet Books, New American Library, 1982), 259–60.
3. Lloyd Ogilvie, *Ask Him Anything* (Waco, TX: Word Books, 1981), quoted in Bob and Michael W. Benson, *Disciplines for the Inner Life* (Waco, TX: Word Books, 1985).
4. Victor Rangel-Ribeiro, *Reader's Digest*, August 1989, 76.
5. Puls, 119.
6. Annie Dillard, *Pilgrim at Tinker Creek* (New York: Harper's Magazine Press, 1974), 276.
7. Louis Evely, *That Man Is You* (New York: Paulist Press, 1964), 121.
8. Henri J. M. Nouwen, "The Prodigal Comes Home," *National Catholic Reporter*, August 4, 1989.

9. *A Man for All Seasons* (1966), screenplay by Robert Bolt, based on his play. *Open Road,* distributed by Columbia Pictures.

10. G. K. Chesterton, *The Fame of Blessed Thomas More* (New York: Sheed and Ward, 1929), 63.

Chapter 11

1. This insight and story of the visit with the Amish family has provided me with a new perception of the "born-again" experience. A previous work of mine, *The Signature of Jesus,* contains this account.

2. May, 192.

3. Nikos Kazantzakis, *Zorba the Greek* (New York: Touchstone, 1996), 300. First published in 1946.

4. Andrew Greeley, *What a Modern Catholic Believes About God* (Chicago: Thomas More Press, 1971), 91–92. Prior to Greeley's career as a novelist, he wrote two books on the theology of the Old and New Testament and revealed a remarkable gift for synthesis.

5. Louis M. Savary and Patricia H. Berne, *Prayerways* (San Francisco: Harper & Row, 1980), 7.

6. Sir Rabindranath Tagore, *Fruit-gathering* XVIII (New York: The Macmillan Company, 1916).

7. De Mello, 39.

A Word After

1. Eugene Peterson, *Traveling Light* (Downers Grove, IL: InterVarsity Press, 1982), 39.

The Scandal Of Grace

1. Sue Monk Kidd, *When the Heart Waits* (San Francisco: Harper San Francisco, 1990), 141.
2. Amy Welborn, January 5 excerpt from *Living Faith* (Fenton, MO: Creative Communications for the Parish, Jan/Feb/Mar 2000).
3. *The Big Book of Alcoholics Anonymous* (New York: AA World Services, 1976), 66–67.
4. John Kavanaugh, *America,* vol. 173, no. 10 (October 7, 1995), 23.
5. Alan Jones, *Soul-Making* (San Francisco: Harper & Row, 1985), 145

The Signature of Jesus
by Brennan Manning

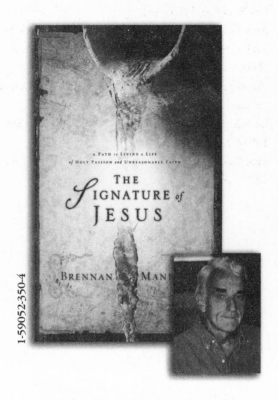

1-59052-350-4

"Behold," Jesus proclaims, "I stand at the door and knock." You may have already met Him at the door...but do you truly *know* Him? Have you been transformed by His furious, passionate, unexplainable love? Join Brennan Manning, the bestselling author of *The Ragamuffin Gospel*, on a personal journey to experience Christ's love and live with His passion.